Switzerland: an International Banking and Finance Center

Max Iklé

Zurich, Switzerland

Translated from the German by **Eric Schiff**

Washington, D.C.

Dowden, Hutchinson & Ross, Inc. Stroudsburg, Pa

Contents

Introduction

Much has already been written about the Swiss banks. The imagination of journalists and writers was naturally stimulated by the fact that in a small country without access to the sea and without raw material deposits, an international financial center could have arisen which today ranks third after New York and London, and in some respects may even have outstripped London. One of these writers, F. T. Fehrenbach, actually succeeded in making a bestseller of his book "The Swiss Banks." In England the book appeared, characteristically, under the title "The Gnomes of Zurich."

The expression "Gnomes of Zurich" originated in England, but it was wrong to attribute it to the former British Minister of Foreign Affairs, Mr. Brown. From the etymological findings of the German linguist Duden we can gather that the word "Gnome" was coined by that famous Swiss physician, natural scientist, theologian, and creative genius in the field of language, Theophrastus Paracelsus, who lived in the 16th century. It is thus not without a certain irony that the nickname which was given to the Swiss banks, may be regarded as a Swiss linguistic creation.

"Gnome" is not an abusive term. Presumably the British, when using the term with reference to the Swiss banks, wish to emphasize primarily the difference in size as between British and Swiss banks, although there may well be in it a certain undertone of anger about the fact that in the last two decades the importance of the Swiss banks has risen steadily, whereas London as a financial center was suffering under the difficulties which the British currency experienced. One should be able to understand this. We shall have to point out later that the Swiss banks and monetary authorities did not have the slightest intention to oust London from its position as the most important financial center of Europe, and that they in fact did all they could to bolster the basis of that position, the British pound. Seeing matters in their true light, we find that there is no such thing as competition between financial centers, since as a matter of fact, they support each other. So there would be little sense in any attempt to compete with London as a financial center, quite apart from the fact that one cannot create centers of finance. They come into being if and when the prerequisites for their existence are present. In the absence of these prerequisites, even the most elaborately organized setup cannot lay the foundations for a financial center.

The sensational reports about Swiss banks allegedly protecting dictators and gangsters through secrecy and numbered accounts are products of newsmen's hunting for sensations. The autochthonous, seasoned Swiss banks are in the habit of taking a good hard look at their clients. There are no anonymous banking accounts. Again and again it has been asserted that leading men of the Third Reich owned funds deposited with Swiss banks, but the existence of these deposits could never be established. One cannot build up a financial center with dictators and members of the underworld as clients. Quite different factors must have been operating. To examine them, and to analyze the origin and the functioning of the Swiss financial center, will be one of the tasks of this study.

1 The Origin of the Swiss Financial Center

1. Historical Background

Switzerland is an Alpine country. Its development and existence is inextricably bound up with its location in the Alps. From time immemorial, populations dwelling among mountains have been inspired by a desire for freedom and independence; this was the case not only in Switzerland, but in neighboring Tyrol as well. These people do not want to be subjects, so the countries Schwyz, Uri, and Unterwalden, refused to tolerate foreign rulers as early as the thirteenth century.

With the opening of the Gotthard pass, the inhabitants of the valleys beneath this vital Alpine passageway moved into the focus of history. The strategic importance of the Alpine passages made it advisable for the potentates of Europe to be on good terms with the people dwelling at the entrance to the Gotthard, who obtained the first Charters from the German Emperors at an early time. But this did not by any means mark the beginning of peaceful development. For more than two centuries the Confederates had to defend their freedom and independence in numerous wars, and it was not until the Peace of Westphalia that their independence was definitely recognized.

Later it was in the interest of the great powers of Europe that the passes across the Alps be in the hands of an independent small nation, for if one great power had taken possession of them, it would have gained a dominant position. Thus Switzerland became the warder of the Alpine passageways, and she has continued in this role of trustee up to the present day even though the strategic importance of the passes has declined.

The Gotthard pass is protected by German-speaking inhabitants of the valleys to the north, and by Italian-speaking people dwelling in the valleys to the south. At the foot of the Great St. Bernard pass we find a French-speaking population, and around the roads leading up to the Graubuenden passes live Romansh-speaking people. A common task and common ideals brought German-speaking, French-speaking, Italian-speaking, and Romansh-speaking Swiss together, first in a loose alliance, and eventually in the Swiss Confederation. The common intellectual outlook proved stronger than the ties by which language linked them to the great cultural centers of Europe.

The bravery of the Swiss warriors was common knowledge in the Middle Ages. Even their few defeats contributed to their fame. In the late Middle Ages it was no longer necessary to defend the independence of the country by force of arms, but the warrior's spirit was still very much alive among the Swiss, and since the homeland could not provide a living for all of its sons, they emigrated in order to serve in foreign armies. At that time there were Swiss regiments on all the battlefields of Europe. The French kings, the German princes, and the Italian dukes thought it highly important to be able to hire Swiss mercenaries. The kings of France and the Popes placed themselves under the protection of Swiss guards on whose loyalty and dependability they could count. At the sack of Rome, on May 6, 1527, the Papal guards defended the Pope, suffering heavy casualties, and in the fight for the Tuileries on August 10, 1792, the Swiss guards had first to be overpowered before the French revolutionaries could lay hands on the king. The retreat of Napoleon's great army at the Berezina proceeded under the cover of Swiss battalions.

On May 20, 1815, at the Vienna Congress, the permanent neutrality of Switzerland was formally recognized as being in the interest of Europe. Up to the present day, this neutrality has been the guideline of Swiss foreign policy. It was respected by the Great Powers in both World Wars. To be sure, neutrality would have remained a dead letter had it not been protected by an efficient army. In relation to her size Switzerland has one of the strongest armies in the world. Within 48 hours an army of more than half a million men armed with modern equipment can be mobilized. Every Swiss must serve in the army. His service as a newly enlisted man lasts four months; then, over a period of eight years, he has to report each year for three weeks' routine military duty. The Swiss citizen army is firmly rooted in the minds of the people. Those who have higher education are as a rule willing to serve longer, with a view to becoming officers. After having gone through his training as a recruit, every Swiss soldier takes his rifle and military equipment to his home. Hardly ever has the weapon been misued for other purposes. This helps to make a swift mobilization possible. In the army the young soldier also gets some education toward his future life as a citizen. The fact that political life in Switzerland is more composed than in most other countries is due in no small measure to the military training the young men receive.

It was against this background that Switzerland as a financial center developed. The country, which for centuries performed the function of trustee in its capacity as a guardian of the Alpine passes, later performed the same function in other capacities. Neutrality, which the surrounding nations recognized and Switzerland protected by force of arms, secured peace for the country, although not without considerable sacrifice. The democratic tradition, which is centuries old, the successful solution of the problems of languages and national minorities, and in recent times, we may well add, the prevailing peace on the labor front, all helped create that atmosphere of confidence which is the most important prerequisite for the rise of a financial center.

2. Geneva as Banking Center

Geneva may well be called the oldest banking center among Swiss cities. This may be connected with the fact that in Basel and Zurich, guild laws hampered economic development. It is true that the Calvinism of Geneva did little to encourage the growth of banking activities—witness the fact that it forbade lending money at interest rates exceeding 6 2/3% at a time when the city of Geneva could raise funds only at 10%. In 1580 an attempt to establish a bank failed, characteristically, because of the objections of pastors. Thus, even in Geneva there was no trace of an autochthonous bank until the middle of the seventeenth century. In 1698 Benedict Turretini was the first to be listed as a banker in notarized records, and by 1709 we find nearly a dozen bankers whose names were to become highly famous in the financial history of Geneva—names such as Tronchin, Saladin, Caladini, Lullin and Marcet, Pictet, Boissier, Mallet, Debary, and Cramer.

During the Spanish War of Succession, Geneva as a financial center was already deeply immersed in the crosscurrents of financial events. The Allies were unable to beat France into submission, for Louis XIV managed again and again to secure the financial means for continuing the war. As suppliers of funds, Amsterdam and Geneva played a significant role. At that time government borrowing existed only in the form of loans with interest in perpetuity; short-term or medium-term financing on the market was still unknown. The banker acted as intermediary between the king and the private money lenders; in this business he operated as an independent contracting party. At the time of

Louis XIV, Samuel Bernard, in particular, was in a key position as a banker as he was in close contact with the French Minister of Finance, Chamillart. During the economic embargo of France, Jaques Henri Huguetan, a French refugee from religious persecution, came to Geneva to ensure continued contact with the Geneva bankers. Huguetan, who stayed in Geneva for two years, was able to obtain a monopolistic position as a fund-raising agent for the French Crown. He raised money at interest rates between 7 and 10%, and lent it out at 10 to 12%. But in many cases even higher profits could be reaped, for the French War Minister was willing to allow up to 35% discount whenever urgently needed funds were placed at his disposal three months earlier than had been agreed upon.

Our information is incomplete concerning the sums of money involved at that time. It has been estimated that the Spanish War of Succession cost the French King 7 million livres a month, nearly one half of which was financed through Geneva over a period of several years.

In 1709 the inevitable financial crisis took place. Bernard, for example, went bankrupt, his balance sheet showing a deficit of 38 million livres.[1] Huguetan had disappeared from Geneva even earlier.

Geneva was hard hit by the insolvency of the royal banker. The banking firm of Lullin and Marcet was the first victim. Many citizens of Geneva, through the intermediary of the firm, had bought bonds issued by Bernard and had invested their savings with the bank. In the spring of 1710 the Geneva Board of Two Hundred suspended those members unable to pay their debts. Among these were names of high standing in Geneva. Many of them subsequently moved to Paris where they thought they had a better chance to defend their claims against Bernard or the Crown. Thus in the years 1714-1716, 44 bankers from Geneva or Switzerland lived in Paris, some of them rising to great prominence later. Nearly all of them were subsequently drawn into the vortex of the John Law transactions.[2]

[1] Stelling-Michaud, Deux aspects du rôle financier de Genève pendant la Guerre de succession d'Espagne, *Bulletin de la Société d'Histoire et d'Archéologie de Genève,* Tome VI, Livraison 2.

[2] The core of John Law's "system" was the foundation of a big colonial company on the English pattern. The company issued shares that could be exchanged against government securities. In this way the whole public debt was to be converted, in due course, into shares of the Société des Indes. The operation went into the history of finance under the name of "Mississippi." At the same time a National Bank, the Banque Royale, was established. It was given the right to issue notes, to collect tax payments, and to administer the public debt. The shares of the Colonial Company were offered on the market in successive issues, first at par, then above par. Their price was driven up so effectively that on November 29, 1719, the total stock was valued on the stock exchange at 4.8 billion livres, while the nominal stock equity was 312 million livres. This could only be achieved by issuing notes in the amount of 1.2 billion livres within a single year. In 1720 when it was found necessary to

Repercussions of the "Law system" on Geneva as a financial center were manifold. Some of the Geneva bankers in Paris ran into difficulties and this had its effects on Swiss firms in Lyon. The banks, to be sure, were fairly well posted by their informers about the events in Paris, with the result that many could in time get rid of the shares of the Société des Indes. But the transfer of the profits that had accrued in Paris encountered difficulties as the value of the French livre in Geneva began to decline. Whereas in January, 1720, the exchange rate of the Geneva currency in relation to the French livre still had been in the neighborhood of 220, it rose to between 1200 and 1300 before August, with the result that book profits were wiped out.

In the years 1720-21 Geneva experienced a full-fledged liquidity crisis. Nobody had enough cash and there were a number of bankruptcies. Reputable merchants had to come to terms with their creditors.

After the Law crisis had been overcome, Geneva as a financial center developed in a satisfactory manner. Not the least important among the contributing factors were the useful contacts the bankers had established all over the world. Many of these "contacts" were Huguenots, with whom ties of family relationship existed. Correspondents, many of whom were themselves natives of Geneva, were kept at all important places. Thus Pan-Cramer wrote in 1763, "Je crois qu'il n'y a pas un coin sur la terre où l'on ne trouve un Genevois." At that time, besides the bankers in Paris, there were three bankers from Geneva in London, and two in Amsterdam, one in Marseille, and one in Lyon.

After 1770 the Geneva banks oriented themselves more and more toward France. In 1785 one could read in a bank bulletin that since 1771 nearly all capital from Geneva had been invested in France. And not all of this capital had its origin in Geneva, some of it had originated in other parts of Switzerland, or even in Germany. In 1789 a banker in Lyon expressed warnings in regard to this too large-scale, one-sided investment.[3]

As has already been mentioned, the French Crown at that time obtained its financial resources mainly by issuing rent-bearing bonds. Originally, rents in perpetuity had dominated the field. Later, rents for life, at interest rates about double those of the rents in perpetuity, came to be used more and more. At first the terms under which the rent could be purchased were made dependent on the purchaser's age; later this principle was replaced by a uniform rent based on the assumption of an average remaining life expectancy of 15 years. By an ingenious device the Geneva bankers managed to turn the obvious weaknesses of the

curb the inflation and to demand supplementary payments from the shareholders, the house of cards collapsed. Only by fleeing to Amsterdam could Law rescue himself from the Bastille, into which his collaborators disappeared. (Luethy Herbert, *La banque protestante en France,* Vol. I, p. 280ff.)

[3] Sayon André, *La banque à Genève pendant les XVIe, XVIIe, et XVIIIe siècles.*

system to their advantage. They picked 30 young girls who had survived infantile diseases and bought French rents on their names. Then they sold these rents to their customers. The healthy climate of Geneva and the hygienic conditions in the city, which were relatively good for those times, contributed to making these Geneva rents particularly attractive. In due course groups of customers who were interested in these rents formed investment partnerships with a view to spreading the risks. The banks were willing to sell the rent-bearing bonds on credit. By signing up for a share in a rent-investment partnership, it was thus theoretically possible without making any payment in cash to acquire a claim to a rent on which one could hope to start collecting actual cash after about 15 years. Around 1780 Geneva's investment in French securities was estimated at more than 100 million livres in Geneva currency, the annual claims for rents amounting to some 12 million livres. So long as one could count on a solvent government and a stable French currency, the system proved to be an excellent business arrangement. But during the American War of Independence, the French Treasury became saddled with a debt so huge that in 1788 rent payments began to slow down. Moreover, there was the decay of the currency. From 1790 to 1794 the exchange rate between the Geneva livre and the French currency unit rose, in fact, from 171 to 500. In 1793 the whole public debt of France was being consolidated into a 5% rent in perpetuity. Owing to the beginning inflation, it lost more and more of its value and, as a result, Geneva moved into a deep financial crisis. The first signs appeared in 1789. An issue in the amount of 20 million livres, which the Geneva banks had taken in as a fixed commitment, could not be sold to the public, and some less seasoned banks that lacked adequate reserves became insolvent. Everybody tried to get rid of the rent-bearing bonds at a time when a reasonable price could still be realized. To finance the rent business, some banks had incurred debt repayable in stable currency. Their clients, however, were no longer in a position to meet their obligations, and so one bank after another defaulted on its payments. The people were quite upset. A search for a culprit set in, and Michel Audéoud, believed to have been the inventor of the so-called "Geneva system," was sentenced to death.

The occupation of Geneva by France in 1798 sharply interrupted the economic development. During the 15 years of French rule, trade, industry, and banking suffered heavily. Reconstruction was not easy. Geneva was cut off from France. The German Customs Union raised new barriers; the textile industry disappeared; only clock and watch making was able to hold its own. The private banks, still the prevailing type in Geneva, financed the export of watches, and they profited from the renewed prosperity of the industry. In 1828, 140 watch manufacturers could be found in Geneva alone. New private banks came into being, many of which have survived up to the present day.[4] Soon the four most prominent banks were operating jointly conducting major business transactions. Their association was named "Quator." Alongside the private banks, other financial institutes arose, such as the Caisse d'Escompte, d'Epargne et de Dépôts in 1789, and in 1816 the Caisse d'Epargne du Canton de Genève, on the pattern of the Bernische Kantonalbank. In the revolution of 1846, James Fazy became a member of the government, and in the years that followed he shaped the fate of Geneva as a financial center. In 1848 he created the Banque de Genève as a Cantonal agency with the right to issue bank notes. Later the bank was transformed into a private institute, with the Canton as the holder of a large portion of the stock. In the same year the Caisse Hypothécaire de Genève came into being. The year 1849 saw the foundation of the Caisse d'Escompte de Genève with a 1-million franc stock equity, and in 1853 Fazy created the Banque Générale Suisse de Crédit International Mobilier et Foncier with a stock equity capital of 25 million francs (only 20% of which was paid in, however)—a universal bank of the type of the French "Banques Mobiliers." But, owing to internal difficulties this ambitiously conceived institute had to be liquidated as early as 1865.

In 1855 the Caisse d'Escompte went out of business and the Comptoir d'Escompte, organized by industrial initiative, with a stock equity capital of 1 million francs (doubled in 1861), took its place.

The Franco-German war of 1870-71 had no adverse effect on the Geneva financial center. Indeed, as a result of the foreign capital flowing into Geneva looking for secure investment opportunities, the banks of Geneva enjoyed considerable prosperity in the ten postwar years. To finance the war indemnity prescribed by the Treaty of Frankfurt, the French Government in the years 1872-73 needed about 5 billion francs. Two fifths of this amount were raised in neutral countries. Geneva was a major participant and this, inevitably, led to some rise in interest rates.

The formation of new banks as joint-stock corporations did not prevent the seasoned private banks from holding their own quite well. This was due in no small measure to the fact that they had a foreign clientele and widespread international contacts. In 1872 the Association Financière grew out of that loose association, the Quator and later, in 1890, it expanded into the Union Financière de Genève. In 1881 several private banks established the Banque Genevoise de Prêts et de Dépôts with a 10-million franc stock equity. This bank also performed the functions of a clearing house and a title search agency. In the middle of the nineteenth century the Geneva stock exchange was created and as

---

[4] *Histoire de la Banque de Genève,* publiée par le Comptoir d'Escompte de Genève, 1931, p. 21.

early as 1860 private banks in Geneva were advising their clients to buy American railroad shares. Side by side with these agencies, financial companies such as the "Omnium Société Civile Genevoise d'emploi de fonds," founded in 1849, appeared on the scene. The "Omnium" invested in various enterprises such as the Channel of Corinth, and in mines in Rio Tinto. The Union Financière de Genève mentioned above, in which ten major private banks had shares, grew into a full-fledged investment trust and spread its financial engagements over a wide field.

Around the turn of the century the expansion of the Comptoir d'Escompte began; as already mentioned, it had been organized in 1861 as an institute to serve the financial needs of industry. In 1898 the stock equity of the Comptoir was raised to 5 million francs. Three further raises brought the stock equity capitalization up to 15 million in 1911. The Institute had been cooperating with French banks since 1906 and at the beginning of World War I it already had the status of a large-scale bank.

3. Swiss Bankers Abroad

The story of the origin of the Swiss financial center would not be complete without a survey of the Swiss bankers and other men of finance who were working in Paris and elsewhere in the eighteenth and the beginning of the nineteenth century.

Bernard, the banker of Louis XIV, had only one serious competitor. That was the banking firm of the three brothers Hogguer. The Höggers, as the name was originally written, were descendants from an old family in St. Gallen. They had migrated to Lyon, where a large Swiss colony, the so-called "Nation Suisse," had settled. In Lyon the people from St. Gallen were at first engaged in the business of selling linen produced in their home town. With the conclusion of the peace treaty with Francis I, trade in linens profited more than any other product from the tariff concessions that had been negotiated in the Treaty. The three brothers Marc-Frédéric, Daniel, and Jean-Jacques, shifted their activities more and more from trade to banking and at the beginning of the eighteenth century they were the owners of a banking firm in Paris. The Höggers succeeded in establishing themselves as suppliers of funds for the King. Essentially, their business transactions consisted in importing silver and having it coined at Strasbourg, Metz, or at some other place where a mint was in operation, with a view to making the coined money available to the King. Considerable profit margins could be earned in such a business. In exchange for the delivered silver coins, the French Crown handed its bankers paper money and short-term bonds, so-called "Assignats"; but only in Paris was the paper money accepted at par value. In Lyon, a "disagio" of 25 percent had to be taken in stride, and after some time the assignats could be traded only at half their nominal value, if at all. Inevitably this created difficulties for the royal bankers who were responsible for the repayment of the funds they had raised to finance the whole business.

But the three Högger brothers were not only the bankers of the French Crown. They also lent considerable sums to Charles XII of Sweden, with the result that they were elevated to the rank of Swedish baronets. Thus we find them later as Baron de Coppet, Marquis de Garo, and Comte de Bignan, the names referring to the castles they obtained. In the financial crisis of 1709 the banking firm of Högger fared no better than Bernard, their competitor. The firm found itself caught in a labyrinth of claims and debts. To disentangle the maze, government commissions were set up. It seems that well-to-do relatives from St. Gallen helped in making the liquidation a smooth procedure. In a way it is surprising that the reputation of the Höggers suffered so little by the events, but, after all, what had brought about the collapse was the King's insolvency and not their own. The liquidation of the first Högger bank was hardly complete when Antoine, the son of Marc-Frédéric, set up a new bank which, notwithstanding the sad experience of the previous generation, again went into the business of financing the Crown. To be known as the banker of the "Roi Soleil" was valued as a supreme achievement by these Protestant republicans of Swiss descent. Antoine Högger's bank placed considerable sums at the disposal of the King, and received paper money and treasury bills in exchange. The whole thing ended in a flood of law suits and confrontations with the Crown and the creditors. Antoine Högger, who had no family, died 1767 in poverty, bitterness in his heart. He had not come to terms with the Crown.

As a young man, Antoine's cousin Jacques-Christophe, a son of Daniel, was sent to Amsterdam. In the relatively quiet climate of this city he was to learn the art of banking under his uncle Rietmann, a man from St. Gallen. In 1722 he set up a bank in Amsterdam. After his death in 1735, his widow carried on the business of the bank; later it was run by his son Daniel who brought several associates into the firm. So the bank appeared under various names, such as Horneca Hogguer, & Co., and later Hogguer, Grand & Co. The bank repeatedly extended loans to Sweden. It was also in the colonial business. After the Grands, who came from the Vaud, had joined the firm as associates, business relations with France were resumed. George Grand's brother Ferdinand, then a banker in Paris, was instrumental in re-establishing the contact. During the American War of Independence the Högger bank in Amsterdam floated loans in behalf of Benjamin Franklin and granted credits to American entrepreneurs. Repayment of these credits met with some difficulties, however. At the beginning of the nineteenth century, Paul Iwan Hogguer, scion of Daniel, attained high positions. In 1840 he became Mayor of Amsterdam and the first President of the Nederlandsche Bank.[5]

Isaac Thellusson went to Paris at an early age to join the staff of the banking firm of Tourton and Guiguer in which he swiftly rose to an executive position. When he was only 28 he was consulted, with other royal counselors, about the prospects of the Law system which was then in its beginnings. He was against Law's plans, and turned out to be one of his strongest opponents. Tourton appointed Thellusson as his sole heir, but he had to fight for his rights under this title in a law suit against Tourton's nephew. In this fight he solicited the help of Geneva, the city of his birth. In this way he once more came into contact with the Geneva authorities who appointed him as their plenipotentiary in Paris. Later François Tronchin, the son of the syndic of Geneva, became his business associate. Although Thellusson's position in the banking firm was only that of limited partner, he actually was the leading man and was held in high esteem in the financial quarters of Paris. In 1733 during the Polish War of Succession, François Tronchin and Company, like the Höggers before, became the suppliers of funds to the French army, and in the crisis year 1738 the French government assigned to Thellusson the important job of the centralized procurement of grain. He performed this job to general satisfaction. François Tronchin's brother Jean-Robert, who until then had run a banking firm in Lyon—he was Voltaire's banker—likewise moved from Lyon to Paris, where he received the highest awards for his services.

Only a few of the numerous Swiss bankers who lived in Paris during the Law period were able to stay in business: ten from Geneva, Ehinguer from Basel, and Labbard from Thurgau. The latter's bank was subsequently taken over by his son-in-law Isaac Vernet. Still later, young Jacques Necker of Geneva and Georges Tobie Thellusson became associates in this banking firm which they ran under the name Thellusson, Necker and Company. Business development was excellent and the bank was considered one of the first institutes of Paris. Necker made a large fortune and became a man of great reputation. In 1768 the city of Geneva appointed him as its representative at the Royal Court, thus making him a member of the diplomatic corps in Paris. In 1772 he retired from active business. The bank was subsequently run by Jean Girardot, Thellusson's brother-in-law, and Louis Necker, Jacques' brother. Later Louis had to take on the name Germany because Jacques Necker did not want his name to appear in the firm and in 1777 Rudolphe-Emanuel Haller, a son of the famous poet and natural scientist Albrecht von Haller, came in. The bank thereafter called itself Girardot, Haller and Company. Necker took to writing and became more and more

[5] Luethy, op. cit., Vol. I, p. 196ff., Vol. II, p. 330ff.

engaged in politics. He criticized Turgot's administration of the finances, and when Turgot had to resign, Necker was called to a post in the Ministry of Finances. The appointment of a foreign-born to such a post was an extraordinary event and a Protestant in such a position meant a challenge to the Church. Never before had a banker been made Minister of Finance. To overcome these difficulties, a stooge was appointed Minister, while Necker was given the title "Directeur Général des Finances." Although Necker succeeded in restoring general confidence in French finances, he did not remain unopposed. One of his opponents was Isaac Panchaud, the son of a Bern family born in London. He had established himself in Paris as a banker, but without great success. He had a certain standing in politics, however, and since he was a financial expert, the door to Turgot was open to him. He was the sponsor of a Caisse d'Escompte, a government agency which was actually set up in the last few weeks of Turgot's rule. The main responsibility of this institute was to be the discounting of commercial bills of exchange. The bank interests us only because on the original board of directors, which consisted of seven men, there were—apart from two government representatives—only Swiss bankers. Besides Panchaud, we find the names Pache (from Geneva), Marck (from Basel), Sellonf (Schlumpf) (from St. Gallen), and Delessert (from Cosonay and Geneva). After Necker had entered the Ministry of Finance, however, the board of directors was enlarged.

Of the other Swiss banks, which in the eighteenth century had a certain importance in Paris, we may mention the Mallet bank. The year 1723 is generally considered to have been the year of its foundation, and so the bank could celebrate its two hundredth anniversary in 1923. The institute was thus one of the oldest and most renowned private banks in Paris.[6] Another banking firm was linked with the names De la Rive, Lullin and Rillier—three old names from Geneva. Less close were the ties that linked the bankers Banquet, Chabert, and Pache to Geneva. Rougemont, a banker from Neuenburg, along with Hottinguer, represented Zurich interests for some time.

4. Basel as Banking Center

Whereas Basel can look back on a longer tradition of capital export than most of the other Swiss cities, banks in the present sense can be found only at relatively late date in the city on the Rhine. There were, to be sure, money changers in early medieval times but the people engaged in this business, which was not considered particularly honorable, were at first mostly Lombards. During the Council of Basel (1431-1449) many foreign money changers came to Basel. At

---

[6] Luethy, op. cit. Vol. II, p. 246ff.

that time even Cosimo Medici had a branch agency in Basel which took care of the money transactions of the Council. In 1533 exchange of money was made an activity reserved to the government, and a public agency was set up which in due course engaged in banking operations of all sorts but encountered strong opposition because of its monopolistic character. In 1746, in the wake of a few ill-fated credit transactions, the enterprise was discontinued.

At the turn of the eighteenth century, so-called "speculation shops"—such as, for example, the firm Merian Brothers—engaged in banking, commission business, and transactions of a speculative nature. They performed all these activities along with commodity trade. The combination of forwarding money and banking was also quite frequent. Another place where we find this combination is St. Gallen, where the private bank Wegelin and Company grew out of the forwarding agency Caspar Zyli. The firm of Merian and Speyr, which had been founded in 1816, at first also carried on banking as a sideline activity within the forwarding business. In 1824 it assumed the name Speyr & Cie and became a private bank altogether. In 1912 it was taken over by the Swiss Bank Corporation. Almost equally old is the bank La Roche, which had risen out of the firm Benedict La Roche (founded 1787).

The present banking firm Zahn and Company grew out of the firm of Bischoff, founded 1806 in St. Alben. Dreyfus Sons and Company, A.G., was founded in 1813 by Isaak Dreyfus. In 1841 J. Riggenbach established himself as a private banker. His firm was later continued in business by A. Sarasin and Company. Luescher and Company trace their existence back to 1855 and E. Gutzwiller and Company to 1886.

Even before the foundation of the Confederation in 1848 and the introduction of the Swiss franc in 1850, Basel had become an important "storehouse" of capital, not only for the rest of Switzerland but for Upper Baden as far as Karlsruhe and Stuttgart, and for eastern France as far as Besançon, Lyon, Strasbourg, and Nancy. In neighboring Alsace the Basel banks, naturally, have a particularly well-established standing; they keep up close mutual business relations with Paris, Lyon, and Frankfurt.

In the year 1862, there were 20 banks listed in the Basel official register (Ragionenbuch) but only nine of them confined themselves to banking. The others were also engaged in other business. In addition to the private banks a few other banking firms were set up in the nineteenth century, such as, in 1809, an institute that called itself "Interest-Bearing Savings," and in 1843, the Clearing and Deposits Bank (Giro-und Depositenbank) which, however, gave way only one year later to the Bank of Basel. Along with other banking activities, the last-named institute issued bank notes. In this line of business the Basel institute occupied a leading place among the banks of issue that existed in Switzerland at the time. When the Swiss National Bank was founded, the Bank of Basel was merged with the Swiss Bank Corporation.

In the middle of the nineteenth century it became evident that if Basel was to maintain its place as a banking center, the private banks would have to cooperate more closely in the issuing business and new, strong banks would have to be established. In fact two groups of private banks were formed. The first, comprising the firms Bischoff, Ehinger, Merian, Passavant, Riggenbach, and Speyr, formed a syndicate in order to spread the risks of the issuing business and to conduct major transactions for common account. The syndicate assumed the name "Bank Corporation" ("Bank-Verein"). In the second group, which was formed somewhat later, we find the names La Roche, Iselin and Staehelin, Oswald Brothers, Luescher, and Dreyfus. In 1862 this group in cooperation with commercial firms founded the first big banking house in the city, the Trade Bank of Basel ("Basler Handelsbank"), with a 20-million franc stock equity, of which 10 million were initially issued. In due course the institute set up branch offices in Geneva, Zurich, and, temporarily, in Bern. Up to the outbreak of World War I, the institute grew into one of the eight big banking houses of Switzerland.

Even after the foundation of the Trade Bank of Basel, the first-named group of banking firms continued the loose form of cooperation that had been contemplated originally. The group had no intention of setting up a new banking house. But after the war of 1870-71, when foreign financial groups made preparations for organizing a bank in Basel with international participation, the syndicate decided to take the initiative and it was a logical proposition that the new institute should be given the name "Bank Corporation of Basel" ("Basler Bankverein").[7] The stock equity was set at 50 million francs, of which 30 million were issued and taken over by the founders as a firm commitment. A bigger banking syndicate, in which foreign institutes were also represented, offered the shares on the market. As a result of the then rampant general economic crisis, the new bank suffered losses in its second year and an adjustment of the stock equity capital became necessary. In 1895 came the merger with the Bank Corporation of Zurich ("Zuercher Bankverein") and two years later the Swiss Union Bank in St. Gallen was taken over, which suggested changing the name of the firm into Swiss Bank Corporation ("Schweizerischer Bankverein"). Foreign business was taken up at an early date and in 1898 a branch opened in London. By absorbing other Swiss banks, Swiss Bank Corporation soon grew into one of the most important of the big banking houses.

The year 1890 brought suggestions from political quarters to set up a public bank. Such a step seemed plausible since in many other cantons institutes of this type were already in existence. But it was not until October 1, 1899, that the Cantonal Bank of Basel ("Basler Kantonalbank") could open its counters.

[7] A. R. Weber, *Basler Bank-und Boersenwesen* (separate reprint from "Wirtschaftsgeschichte Basel").

Besides other banking transactions, the Cantonal Bank issued bank notes during the following period up to the formation of the Swiss National Bank.

5. Zurich as Banking Center

As a banking center Zurich made its appearance at a relatively late date. At the beginning of the eighteenth century when Geneva was already in the thick of European financial transactions, we do not find any bank in Zurich in the full meaning of the word. The Zurich of that time was a small town of 10,000 inhabitants. To be sure, even Zurich lent money in medieval times. These money transactions were frequently connected with payments due to Swiss mercenaries. Thus we know of a loan granted by Zurich in 1570 to Charles IX, who after the peace treaty of St. Germain dismissed Swiss mercenaries but did not have the funds to pay what was still owed them. Zurich at that time granted a loan of 50,000 crowns (150,000 livres) at 5% for two years. Bern and Freiburg together made 70,000 crowns available. Frequently, also, the municipal loans were connected with the salt trade, the municipal Salt Office functioning as money lender. In the Thirty Years' War a few loans were granted to borrowers in southern Germany; private money lenders also were active in such transactions. At the end of the seventeenth century capital export from Zurich seems to have come to a standstill for quite some time. But general well-being finally increased and the municipal treasury began accumulating funds whose investment met with difficulties even in this early phase. In 1679 the city council for the first time issued an injunction against lowering the rate of interest from 5% to 4%. Nevertheless, the interest rate declined to 3%. In 1730 the idea of establishing a bank turned up for the first time. Requests for loans were flowing in from outside at an increasing rate, but the city maintained an attitude of great restraint. Unlike Geneva, Zurich did not participate in the financing of the Spanish War of Succession. Only the Salt Office granted occasional loans.

The surplus in the municipal treasury of Zurich continued piling up, however, and in 1726 investment of capital in England was contemplated for the first time. As early as 1709 Bern had invested about 1 million Taler in England and Holland. In 1727 the Council of Zurich followed this example by investing 100,000 guilders in English government securities and buying 20 shares of the South Sea Company. These foreign investments originating in Zurich amounted, however, to only 10% of those engaged in by Bern. The intermediary in these transactions was Holzhalb, a Zurich banker established in London who, however, became bankrupt soon afterwards.

In the year 1750 a commission submitted an opinion to the council expressing the view that the rate of interest could not be stabilized by government decree. In 1751 an "Interest Commission" came into being, which was assigned the business of accepting funds as deposits and investing them abroad. In 1755 the job of carrying out these transactions was delegated to a separate new organization which was given the name Leu and Company (after Mr. Leu, the city treasurer), although in actual fact it was strictly a government agency. Leu and Company issued bonds bearing 3 to 3½% interest. These bonds went into the portfolios of Zurich citizens; their value rose from 60,000 R ("Rheinische Gulden") in 1755 to 2,688,000 R in 1797. In its investment policy the commission exercised utmost care. The funds were invested in Austria and later in France. The commission did grant loans to Central and North America, and it lent money to Geneva bankers who, as we have seen, needed funds for their speculative transactions. Otherwise, however, loans raised inland were the exception.

If we disregard a short-lived attempt in 1652 to set up a municipal discount house, we cannot find a bank in Zurich until the middle of the eighteenth century. The merchants of Zurich concentrated on the textile trade without themselves engaging in the banking transactions connected with that trade. They obviously used the services of foreign banks. In the eighteenth century, however, some citizens of Zurich did begin to engage in certain credit transactions. Bonds bearing 3 to 3½% interest were in circulation. Even the craft guilds were occasionally active as money lenders. In the second half of the eighteenth century we find a few business men who could be called "merchant-bankers." The first of them may well have been H. C. Escher, who accepted funds as deposits and then invested them in securities. This enterprise collapsed, however, in 1788. There were other firms that conducted money transactions along with commodity trade. They negotiated, among other things, a loan to Copenhagen. Credits were also granted to Geneva bankers, and every now and then somebody ventured into speculative transactions with French securities.

In Zurich the first private bank in the full sense of the word is the firm Usteri, Ott, Escher and Company. It was founded in 1786 by six Zurich firms which, however, failed to endow the bank with sufficient equity capital. Operation of a branch in Paris was entrusted to the bankers Rougemont and Hottinguer. In the first few years the bank enjoyed a good rating as a financial institute; deposits came flowing in even from Basel. But the representatives in Paris were unable to escape the speculation fever that was raging there and so they ran into losses. From 1800 to 1803 one after the other of the partners got into financial difficulties. The bank had to compound with the creditors and in 1803 it was liquidated. Hottinguer, one of the guilty in the collapse, left Paris and stayed in America for some time. But after his return in 1797, he became Talleyrand's financial adviser, and during the Napoleonic era he was a banker of great standing.[8]

[8] H. C. Peyer, *Von Handel und Bank im alten Zuerich*, p. 144 ff.

But even the city treasury and the interest commission Leu and Company had to take losses on their foreign investments. Toward the end of the eighteenth century, Leu and Company were no longer in a position to pay interest on their bonds. In the autumn of 1798 a general assembly of bondholders took notice of the state of affairs and instructed the commission to liquidate, with as little loss as possible, the foreign investments. At that time only about 20% of the bonded debt, which then amounted to 2.6 million Zurich gulden, was covered by liquid assets, but it was hoped that in the course of a gradual, cautiously moving liquidation, this percentage could be raised to between 50 and 55%. The bonds were declared nonredeemable; repayment was to proceed in installments. For the time being no new bonds were issued. In 1803 the worst seemed over. Some assets could again be sold, though only at a loss. Investments abroad were reduced from 2.7 million to 700,000 gulden in 1822. From then on the business gradually shifted to the homeland. In this way Leu and Company became a private mortgage institute in Zurich.[9]

Around 1805 we find in the official register of Zurich seven firms that called themselves banks, but only two of them, H. C. Escher Son, and Tauenstein, confined themselves to banking. The others were combined enterprises of the kind that existed in other cities as well. As late as 1837, only Tobler-Stadler is listed in the newly introduced official register ("Ragionenbuch") as a bank in the strict sense, side by side with four firms that were combining banking and exchange transactions with commodity trade or silk manufacture. At that time trade in bills of exchange, including foreign bills, was the most important line of business in banking. Since the large-scale firms engaged in the silk and cotton trade were well endowed with capital and performed the money transactions connected with their business themselves, only a limited field of activity remained for the Zurich private bankers. This explains why in Zurich, contrary to what is true of Geneva and Basel, almost no really old, long-established bank can be found. Only the banking firm Rahm and Bodmer can trace its origins back to the beginning of the nineteenth century. It grew out of the firm Caspar Schulthess sel. Erben and Schinz, which existed as early as 1805.

After the Confederation had been founded, Zurich moved into the foreground as an economic and financial center. The growing industrialization and the building of railroad lines called for the setting up of financial institutes of larger size. The Swiss publisher C. Hirzel in Leipzig suggested in 1856 that a branch of the Allgemeine Deutsche Kreditanstalt be established in Zurich. This proposal, however, was not exactly welcome in Zurich. Alfred Escher, the strongest personality in economic and political life at the time, then took the initiative of founding the Swiss Credit Bank (Schweizerische Kreditanstalt) with

[9] Leu und Company, 1755-1955 (memorial).

18

a 15-million franc stock equity capital, and German participation, amounting to 50%, was gladly accepted. The founders reserved 3 million for themselves and offered the remaining 4½ million for public subscription. The success was extraordinary. Whereas 4½ million had been expected, subscriptions reached 218 million. Thus the young banking institute, supported by public confidence, swiftly gained in stature. Escher became the first chairman. He was also the initiator of the Gotthard railroad, an enterprise that was beyond Swiss potentialities and could only be realized with foreign participation. The Swiss Credit Bank played a leading part in the foundation of firms such as Swiss Rent Institute (Schweizerische Rentenanstalt), Swiss Reinsurance (Schweizerische Rueckversicherung), the Machinery Factory Oerlikon, and the Industrial Society for Schappe in Basel. (Schappe is a by-product of silk manufacture.) In 1890 the bank was already in the international business. By way of investment it was interested in the Bank for Oriental Railroads, in the Swiss-Argentine Mortgage Bank, and in other financial companies and in joint action with AEG (Allgemeine Elektrizitaets-Gesellschaft) it established in 1895 the Bank for Electrical Enterprises (Bank fuer elektrische Unternehmungen), known today as "Elektro-Watt."

In Winterthur, the Bank of Winterthur was formed in 1862. Leading men of the Winterthur economy were on the board of directors. The initial stock equity was 5 million; the shares, offered for public subscription, were vastly oversubscribed. The Bank of Winterthur operated predominantly as a trade bank without, however, neglecting other lines of banking. From the start it also ran a warehouse. In addition the bank was active in railroad financing; there, however, it incurred losses, as a result of which the share capital, which in the meantime had been raised to 15 million francs, had to be reduced in 1886 to the former level of 10 million. Concurrent with this measure, preferred shares were issued. After the bank had gained a foothold in various places by way of investments, it merged in 1912 with the Bank of Toggenburg, which had originated in the year 1863 and had established a good name for itself in eastern Switzerland. Out of the merger grew a new big banking house, the Union Bank of Switzerland (Schweizerische Bankgesellschaft).

In 1892 the Federal Bank (Eidgenoessische Bank) moved its headquarters to Zurich. It had been founded in 1863 on the initiative of two Paris banks, the Société Générale de Crédit Industriel et Commercial and the Société Anonyme des Dépôts et de Comptes-Courants. At that time it caused quite a stir that Jakob Staempfli, a member of the Federal council, and like Alfred Escher one of the most prominent politicians of his time, was willing to retire from the Federal council and take the post of chairman of the bank. Stock equity was set at 60 million francs, one half of which had to be subscribed at the time of foundation. Of the 60,000 shares offered at 500 francs per share, 12,000 were taken by

Swiss investors and 18,000, by the French founding banks. By public subscription 11,200 shares could be placed in Switzerland and 18,800 in France. The sum paid in amounted to 20%. In the first ten years, branches were already being set up in St. Gallen, Lausanne, Zurich, Geneva, Lucerne, Basel and La Chaux-de-Fonds. So the bank had the character of a large all-Swiss banking institute when it moved to Zurich.

After the establishment of the Zurich stock exchange in December, 1876, and the publication of the Stock Exchange Act of 1883, the private brokers, who up to that time had taken care of the trade in securities, gradually disappeared. They were replaced by "Effektenagenten" (firms admitted to the stock exchange as licensed brokers). By the Stock Exchange Act of 1886 even commercial banks could be admitted to the stock exchange as agents in this capacity. By 1896, it had 23 firms admitted—20 "Effektenagenten" and 3 joint-stock banks were active there. It was not until 1898 that the Swiss Credit Bank applied for the stock exchange license. The joint-stock company Leu and Company did so only in 1910.

6. Times of War and Crisis

Before the outbreak of World War I, Switzerland had already grown into an international financial center of some importance. Six big banks were in possession of a rather tightly knit network of branches all over Switzerland. The six were the Swiss Credit Bank, Swiss Bank Corporation, Union Bank of Switzerland, Trade Bank of Basel, Federal Bank, and Swiss People's Bank (Volksbank). It was no longer appropriate to speak of segregated financial centers within the country. As a financial center, Switzerland had become an integrated whole, with Zurich, Basel, and Geneva functioning as centers of gravitation and Zurich moving more and more into the foreground with four big banks—the Swiss Credit Bank, Union Bank of Switzerland, Federal Bank, and Leu and Company, A. G. The insurance business, too, was well represented in Zurich (Swiss Reinsurance Company, "Zurich" General Accident and Liability Insurance Company). Firms having their headquarters in Basel were the Swiss Bank Corporation, Trade Bank of Basel, Life Insurance Company of Basel, and the Fire Insurance Company of Basel. The Swiss People's Bank had its headquarters in Bern. In Geneva the Comptoir d'Escompte was about to grow into the dimensions of a big bank; the Geneva private bankers, with their long tradition and their international clientele, also formed an essential part of the Swiss financial center. Each year the banks floated some international loans. Thus we find the following issues in the Almanac of 1912:

4%	German Reich Loan
4%,	Prussian Consols
4%,	Italian Treasury Notes per 1917
4%,	Danish Government Loan 1912
4½%,	Gold Bonds of the City of Moscow
4½%,	Debentures, Central Mortgage Bank of Hungarian Savings Associations
4½%,	Bonds, Anatolian Railroad Company, Third Series
5%,	Gold Debentures, Chicago Rock Island and Pacific Ry. Co. 1932
7%,	Adj. Mortgage Bonds, Denver & Rio Grande R.R. Co.
5%,	Bonds, Virginian Ry. Co. 1957
4½%,	20 Year Convertible Bonds, Baltimore and Ohio R.R.
5%,	I. Mortg. Portland Railway Light and Power Co.
4½%,	Bonds, Siemens Elektrische Betriebe A.G.
5%,	I. Lien ref. Mge. Bonds, Bethlehem Steel Corporation
6%,	Notes Utah Co. per 1917
6%,	Cum. Pref. Stock Amer. Water Works Guarantee Co., Pittsburgh
7%,	Cum. Pref. Stock and Comm. Stock B.F. Goodrich Co.
7%,	I. Pref. Stock Loose Wiles Co.
7%,	Pref. Shares Emerson Brantingham Co.
7%,	Cum. Pref. Stock California Petroleum Corporation United States Motor Company Reorganization Syndicate
7%,	Pref. Stock Moline Plow Co. Common Stock M. Rumely Co.
7%,	Cum. Pref. Stock New Motor Cab Co., Ltd.

Those financial companies that were active in international business, such as Swiss Bank for Capital Investment, Swiss Company for Electric Industry, Bank for Electrical Enterprises, and others, were likewise relying on the market. Swiss banks acted as intermediaries in securing foreign titles on behalf of their customers. Since the supply of Swiss securities suitable for investment was inadequate, American stocks and bonds could be found in every major portfolio. Industry had begun to set up affiliated companies abroad and insurance companies were active in foreign markets from Russia to the United States. Important transit trade companies such as Volkart Brothers in Winterthur and the Trade Bank of Basel already had a widespread network of branches in many regions of the world, India and Africa among them.

To illustrate the degree of international interlocking of interests, we may mention the wide field in which Carl Abegg-Auer, then President of the Swiss Credit Bank, was active. Among other things, he was chairman of the Board of Directors of the Bank for Oriental Railroads (a company financing railroads in the Balkan countries); president of the Bank for Electrical Enterprises; chairman

of the Board of Supervisors of the Electric Power Company of Strasbourg, of the
S. A. de Filature de Schappe in Lyon, and of the Swiss-Argentine Mortgage
Bank. He was a member of the Boards of Directors of the Railway Company
Saloniki-Monastir, the Baghdad Railway, the Compania Barcelonesa de Elec-
tricidad, the German-Overseas Electrical Company (Deutsche-Ueberseeische
Elektrizitaetzgesellschaft), the Banca Commerciale Italiana and the Dollfus, Mieg
and Company, Mulhouse.

The outbreak of World War I set an abrupt end to this development.
Financial and trade relations were disrupted and Switzerland was cut off from
the world market. Import and export became dependent on the good will of the
belligerent nations. Owing to their close connection with neighboring Germany
and Austria, the financial centers Zurich and Basel were more severely affected
than Geneva. The collapse of the German and Austrian currencies resulted in
enormous losses to the banks and their clientele. For a long time people were
unwilling to believe that the German mark was headed for an irreparable
breakdown; the hope that it would recover after the war died hard. Especially
hard hit were banks that had invested in mortgages in Germany, such as Leu and
Company and some smaller institutes in eastern Switzerland.

The consequences of World War I were bitter. According to estimates of that
time, Swiss assets abroad dwindled from 8 to 2.5 billion. The country was
flooded by cheap commodities from abroad, causing the balance of trade to
show a substantial deficit. The markets for short-term money, as well as the
market for long-term capital, lost much of their ability to function in an
efficient manner. The Confederation and a few cities found themselves in the
necessity to raise loans in foreign countries. Thus Pictet and Company, jointly
with Lee Higginson and Company, Boston, negotiated three loans for the
Confederation: 15 million dollars at 5% for one to five years; 30 million dollars
at 5½% for ten years, and 25 million dollars at 8% for 20 years. The Credit Bank
jointly with Morgan and Company negotiated a medium-term loan of 20 million
dollars at 5%, and one having a longer term, amounting to 30 million dollars, at
5½%. Zurich and Bern likewise raised loans in dollars.

The reparations problem, laying heavily upon Germany, prevented a rebound
of her economy, and this had a crippling effect on all of Europe. When the
Dawes Plan (August 1924) and the Young Plan (June 7, 1929) had gone into
effect, it was believed that a solution for the difficult reparation problem had
been found. This contributed to the rise of a new optimism and to a revitalizing
of business.

International financial transactions were resumed. The banks granted credits
to foreign commercial and industrial firms and to German banks. In connection
with the stabilization of the French franc under Poincaré 1926-27, France was

granted a loan, followed shortly afterwards by another loan, this time for the French State Railroad, amounting to 150 million francs at 7%. Both loans were floated by the Credit Bank; both were helpful in the stabilization of the French currency.

Even banks that formerly had not been active in international business, or had entered it only on a few occasions, now participated in it, developing a good deal of initiative. This is true of the Federal Bank, the People's Bank, the Trade Bank of Basel, and the Comptoir d'Escompte. The last-named bank continued its expansion and set up numerous branches, the aim being to become an all-Swiss bank with headquarters in Geneva.

It was not sufficiently realized how weak the foundations were on which the international financial structure and the system of currencies rested. Short-term claims in international finance totaled 55 billion dollars, and many short-term funds were sunk in long-term investments, contrary to the golden rule of banking.

The stock market crash in New York 1929 marked the beginning of the depression of the thirties. The international financial structure broke down. The project of a customs union between Germany and Austria led to withdrawals of funds from Austria. Not long after this, the Austrian Credit-Anstalt collapsed; it suspended payments on May 11, 1931. A chain reaction was thus set in motion, and the run on German banks forced the Darmstaedter and Nationalbank to close its counters on June 13, 1931. The German government decreed a bank moratorium and put the first foreign exchange restrictions into effect. Next, the spark of crisis hit Britain, whose currency after the war had been stabilized, in a somewhat too optimistic mood, at prewar parity. The pound was severed from gold and was devalued. Whereupon one European country after the other tried, by devaluing its currency, to shift to others the unemployment from which it was suffering. In 1933 even the American administration found that it had to give up the fixed parity of the currency unit. At the beginning of 1934 the dollar was devalued by 41%. The repercussions of the crisis in currencies, finance, and general economic conditions were catastrophic. The number of unemployed in Europe went up to millions. The world economy was being shackled by import and foreign exchange restrictions and capital sought refuge in those countries where the risk of devaluation was least. The currency system of the postwar period was a shambles. Hitler recruited his party members out of the armies of unemployed persons in Germany.

France, the Netherlands, and Switzerland, the last remaining members of the gold block, were still clinging to their parities. Switzerland tried in vain to lower the price level by a deflationary policy with a view to regaining her full competitive strength on the world markets. The debility from which export business was suffering could not be overcome and in the middle of the thirties the volume of Swiss exports dwindled to 800 million francs. Unemployment became rampant. The world no longer believed that the gold-block countries could successfully defend their currencies, so a withdrawal of deposits set in. In 1936 when the French government informed the Federal Council that it was under the necessity of devaluing the French franc, the Swiss government, too, though with a loaded heart and only after long deliberation, decided to take the Swiss franc off gold and to devalue it by 30%.

As a result of the devaluation foreign capitals began flowing in again and the situation on the markets for short-term and long-term funds became easier. But the time remaining until the outbreak of World War II was too short to allow the economy to regain its strength.

The international credit and currency crises placed the banks under a burden of extraordinary weight. In the postwar era financial communications with Germany had again been working well. After the experience with the inflation, German investors came to regard deposits in Switzerland as a protection in case times should get worse. Considerable sums were flowing from Germany into Switzerland. For lack of adequate investment opportunities in the homeland, the Swiss banks invested these funds in Germany. Credits to first-rate German firms, or mortgages with gold clauses on good real estate, were considered to be absolutely sound investments. So it was not at all uncommon for the German assets of a Swiss bank to attain or even to exceed the level of its stock equity capital. Hence the German bank moratorium of 1931, and the general transfer moratorium of 1933, hit the Swiss banks at a vital spot. What should be done if the German deposits with Swiss banks were withdrawn while at the same time Swiss assets in Germany were frozen? One solution, to be sure, might have come up for consideration, and was in fact recommended to the Swiss authorities a few times: Switzerland, in her turn, could have ordered a limited moratorium, thus offsetting frozen claims by frozen liabilities. But this would have been against all tradition. The Swiss banks, in fact, subsequently liquidated without fail all deposits their German customers wanted to withdraw, although the banks could no longer liquidate their own assets in Germany. This amounted to a test of strength that is hard to conceive of today. In the years 1930-36 deposits with the large banks as recorded in their balance sheets shrank from 6.6 to 3.2 billion. It is almost a miracle that the banking system could survive this bloodletting. For some banks, to be sure, financial reconstruction became inevitable. All banks that had been active in international business, with the exception of two big ones, had to reduce their stock capital. The Comptoir d'Escompte, for which financial reorganization had become necessary as early as 1931 (its name was then changed to Swiss Discount Bank), as well as the Swiss People's Bank, had to apply for financial assistance from the Federal government which shortly before had organized the Federal Loan Agency (Eidgenoessische Darlehenskasse) for such emergencies. But the Swiss Discount Bank could not be saved and the People's Bank had to undergo a second financial reconstruction. A new Banking Act was put into effect in 1935. The new act granted banks in distress the right to postpone their due dates, and numerous banks subsequently made use of this privilege. In retrospect we may perhaps say that the authorities and the banks, by choosing this difficult course, have made a significant contribution to Switzerland's reputation as a financial center. This reputation has proved its justification in a critical period.

In fact the Swiss banks and authorities did their best to safeguard financial interests in these difficult times. In September, 1931, the first standstill agreement between Swiss and German banks was concluded. After the announcement of the general transfer moratorium, which entailed heavy sacrifices for the creditors of Germany, Switzerland attempted to keep her creditor rights effective by introducing bilateral clearing with Germany. In this attempt she was in a strong position inasmuch as her commodity trade with Germany steadily produced import surpluses, so that there was enough scope, within the framework of a clearing agreement, for the accrual of interest on the Swiss claims. This brought some relief, even though capitals remained frozen.

World War II did not find Switzerland unprepared. At the peak of the crisis in 1936 the Defense Loan was issued. It was oversubscribed, despite an interest rate of 3% which of course involved a sacrifice. The Swiss people wanted thereby to enable the Federal Council to speed up armaments in view of the threatening clouds on the political horizon. Thus a reorganized and re-equipped army could occupy the frontiers of the country in 1939. The costs of national defense reached 8.2 billion francs, and during the war years the Federal debt, despite introduction of new taxes, rose from 2.3 to 8.7 billion. However, the financing of the deficit was done primarily by way of long-term loans. Credit by the bank of issue was used only quite temporarily, so that inflation could be kept within relatively narrow bounds.

Surrounded as she was by the Axis powers, Switzerland had trouble in her attempt to uphold her foreign trade. As commodity shipments from Germany declined more and more, an export surplus arose in the clearing agreement with Germany which at the end of the war reached the billion level. The country was also hard hit by the action the United States took in freezing her dollar accounts which amounted to 6 billion francs. Financial transactions with the United States thus came to a standstill. Considerations connected with the fight against inflation motivated the National Bank to accept at the official rate only those dollars originating in commodity trade. This created a "finance dollar" which at times showed a substantial disagio. An affidavit was introduced for purposes of transactions with England, the aim being to make the continuation of interest payments possible, at least to some extent.

7. *After World War II*

The second World War left a pile of rubble so vast it can hardly be imagined. The German economy was prostrate. As clearing payments came to a halt, those foreign assets of Swiss banks that were located in Germany, Austria, or in East European countries could no longer be entered as assets in the balance sheets. This forced two large banks, the Trade Bank of Basel and the Federal Bank, to transfer their Swiss assets and liabilities to stronger institutes and to carry on as "truncated banks" ("Rumpfbanken") managing only their foreign assets, which had become so problematical. It is true that the Swiss economy emerged intact out of World War II, but only a very few lines of business drew any profit from the war.

It was generally expected that the transition from the war economy to a peace economy would be accompanied by crisis and unemployment in a manner similar to what had happened after World War I. The Federal government was prepared, if necessary, to adopt a comprehensive program to create new employment opportunities. But first it tried to overcome the critical period by promoting exports. This course suggested itself all the more as there was a serious dearth of commodities in all of Europe, a dearth that could not be filled owing to the prevailing scarcity of foreign exchange. This is why so-called "Swing Credits" were provided in the trade and payment agreements of the postwar era. The purpose was to work out a setup under which the volume of exports would not depend on the volume of imports, as it had under the clearing agreements of the interwar period. France and Britain, in particular, used these credits in full; in 1948 they totaled 680 million francs. In this way the transition to a peacetime economy could be achieved without any setbacks.

The banks in their turn granted credits to foreign countries, especially France and Belgium. In part these credits financed Swiss exports, in part they helped in providing the homeland with some necessities, as did a credit to "Montecatini" in Milan and one to the "Charbonnages de France." These two credits were repaid by successive deliveries of electricity (in the first case) and of coal (in the second case). After 1947, one could again contemplate—only with hesitation at first—the floating of loans abroad, Belgium being the main borrower in the initial phase.

Following an initiative of the United States, the European countries formed the OECE (Organisation Européene de Coopération Economique), in the frame of which the European Payments Union was set up in 1950. This Union may well be called the most constructive part of the great Marshall Plan.

Various Swiss organizations, such as Swiss Help (Schweizer Hilfe) and Help for Europe (Europa-Hilfe), donated gifts, and a broad stream of food parcels flew across the frontier. The Swiss contribution to the reconstruction of Europe after the war, including the Federal credits, attained a level which, on a per head of population basis, could certainly match the American Marshall Plan.

In 1948 Germany carried out her currency reform, which was the basis for the reconstruction of the German economy. But the European currency situation was by no means settled as yet. In 1949 Britain, taking account of the depreciation the pound had experienced as a result of the war, decided to devalue her currency by 30%. Within one week, 26 other countries followed suit. Nearly all of Switzerland's most important trade partners, with the exception of the United States, devalued their currencies, most of them in the same proportion as Britain had done. What was Switzerland to do in this situation? This writer still has a vivid recollection of the decisive meeting that took place in the Department of Finances, with Mr. Nobs of the Federal government as chairman. Voices could be heard from eastern Switzerland to the effect that the textile industry would be losing its ability to compete if the existing parity were maintained. The speakers of the National Bank came out for maintenance of the existing parity, and in the Department of Finances, too, hope was expressed that it would be possible to avoid devaluation, provided this could be justified from a general economic point of view. In this debate the vote of the delegate of the Swiss Trade and Industry Association proved decisive. He forcefully emphasized that in view of the strong demand for goods that was still widespread abroad, Switzerland could stick to the existing parity. Thus a unanimous resolution, later approved by the Federal Council, was adopted. The course chosen proved to be correct. Although business activity did slow up a bit, the Swiss economy retained its competitive strength. The price level subsequently declined somewhat, and this made it possible to abolish the subsidies that had been introduced to make consumer purchases less expensive.

During the war period and in the immediate postwar era the Western powers had little understanding of Switzerland's policy of neutrality. Thus the country was put under strong American pressure in the course of the Morgenthau policy. The United States demanded that Switzerland seize the German accounts and other assets in the country in order to make the proceeds available for reparation payments. This was a serious matter for a nation that had always stood for protection of private property. The tiresome negotiations eventually led to a compromise that was acceptable even to the German owners of those assets.

Once more Switzerland had impressively asserted her role as a trustee. Nowhere in the world could the German owners of property located in other countries achieve a more favorable settlement.

Further difficult problems arose in connection with the efforts to realize Swiss claims vis-à-vis foreign countries. At the end of the war the claims of the Federal Government originating in the clearing arrangements amounted to 1 billion francs; they seemed unrecoverable. At the beginning of the fifties, an agreement about Swiss accounts could be concluded with Italy. Of the accounts representing claims of the Confederation, 60% were recognized.

After the German currency reform had been accomplished in 1948 but before termination of the regime of occupation, the Allies were interested in settling the question of the German debts. The Swiss would have preferred to tackle this difficult problem at a later time. But the timing was fixed by the Allies, who in 1952 sent out invitations to a conference in London about settlement of the German debts. Switzerland, as the third largest creditor, had to participate. The attempt to place the so-called "clearing billion" on the agenda met with great obstacles, however. The United States, Britain, and France, wished to discuss only the prewar and postwar debts. Those debts that had arisen during the war should be left aside because their inclusion in the talks would have prejudged the reparation problem. The Swiss delegates, however, were determined to settle the question of the "clearing billion" within the framework of the London conference. After long preliminary talks, the claim originating in the clearing was eventually admitted on the agenda, as the Swiss delegates would otherwise have left the conference. In subsequent negotiations in Bern, the German delegate offered a bare 50 million francs in settlement of the "clearing billion." The Swiss delegates demanded 600 million, in analogy with the result that had been worked out with Italy. After negotiations that lasted for months, 500 million francs were eventually agreed upon. For the German partner in the negotiations, acceptance of the compromise was made easier by Switzerland declaring her willingness to reinvest 100 million in the German Federal Railroads, to finance the electrification of the important connecting line Karlsruhe-Basel. Besides the "clearing billion," a number of secondary claims, amounting to 180 million francs, had to be settled. Because Switzerland's position as a negotiating party was even more difficult here, the Swiss delegates stated right at the outset that Switzerland would be willing to invest an amount to be agreed on in the German steel industry with the understanding that another agreement, to be concluded simultaneously, would provide for German deliveries of steel whenever this product became scarce. In the definitive agreement the amount was eventually set at 150 million, of which 110 million were invested in the steel industry and 40 million in the German Federal Railroads. Apart from their importance for the steel industry and the

German Railroads, these reinvestments had a positive psychological impact. The fact that Switzerland was prepared to grant credits to the German economy, which at that time was still run down, evoked great interest in and outside of Germany.

Acceptable compromises could be negotiated in London about the private claims as well. Indemnities for nationalizations were agreed on with some East European countries. Thanks to the clearing agreements concluded with these countries, the indemnities could be successively realized. Financial settlement with Eastern Germany was not achieved, however.

Within the framework of the European Payments Union, which provided for a multilateral clearing, the surplus countries had to grant to the deficit countries credits amounting, on the average, to 50% of their surplus balances. In view of the economic situation the German Federal Republic in its first few years saw fit to draw on the EPU credits to a considerable extent. As a result other countries, Switzerland among them, became creditors. The Swiss claim threatened to reach the billion level in a few years. Ways and means were therefore being sought to limit it.

When the agreement with Germany about the reinvestment of clearing balances had become known, the French State Railroad had something to say. It pointed out that the railway line Karlsruhe-Basel, which in a way was competing with French lines, was favored by the impending electrification, and the French inquired about the possibility of a Swiss credit for the electrification of French connecting lines. As the Swiss Federal Railways supported the request, the Federal Council declared its willingness to grant the credit, provided it would be handled through EPU. This meant a corresponding reduction of the Swiss creditor position within the Payment Union. The credit transaction was, in fact, carried through in this manner. Not much time passed before the Italian State Railroad, too, put out a feeler. Although the direct line leading up to the Gotthard Pass was already electrified, there were various lines on the way to the Simplon Pass which the Swiss Federal Railroads were interested in electrifying. Moreover, a large number of unsolved questions between Switzerland and Italy were still open, and these could be settled in the course of the credit negotiations. This credit, amounting to 200 million francs, was likewise handled through EPU, with a view to reducing the creditor position of Switzerland. At the end of this series of credits stood Austria, which obtained a credit of 55 million for further development of the Arlberg railroad line. In this way a network of electrified railway approaches, which greatly contributed to transit traffic through Switzerland, came into being.

Private capital export also began flowing again. From 1947 to 1955 loans to foreign borrowers, amounting to 1.7 billion, were floated on the Swiss market.

By setting up investment trusts, the Swiss banks gave a strong impetus to

29

capital export. In ever-increasing measure foreign portfolios were entrusted to these banks, which had a long history of managing foreign property.

Foreign banks established demand deposits and time deposits with Swiss banks. As there was no domestic money market of adequate absorbing capacity, the banks reinvested these funds abroad. After convertibility had been restored in 1959, the interdependence between the Swiss banking system and foreign economies increased more and more. In the postwar period, foreign firms and financial groups decided to establish holding companies in Switzerland in order to control their European affiliated companies from there. The central location of the country, the convertibility of its currency, the fact that several languages were spoken there, all favored the development described.

Similar considerations induced foreign financial groups to set up financial companies and banks in Switzerland. In this way Switzerland grew into the role of an international financial center, although this goal had not been consciously aimed at.

The history of the Swiss financial center is very instructive in several respects. It shows, first of all, that Switzerland's role as a financial center is not an accidental result of postwar developments, but is built on an old tradition of capital export. At the same time, the historical record shows that the export of capital, viewed over this long time span, moved in waves, with many setbacks and disappointments. We have seen that there was a substantial capital export at the beginning of the eighteenth century during the Spanish War of Succession, and in another period at the end of that century until the Napoleonic era put an end to this development. In the nineteenth century Switzerland at first became a capital importing country. The construction of railways and the establishment of banks could be financed only by drawing foreign capital into the country; the growing Swiss industry absorbed to a large extent the capital that had been formed at home. It was not until after the war of 1870-71 that some capital export came to life again, and only toward the end of the century did the stream broaden. After World War I, Switzerland once more saw fit to import capital. But it would appear that capital exports exceeded imports as early as the middle of the twenties. These findings are of interest because they show that the flow of capital, unlike the flow of goods, changes direction only slowly. This is not without importance for an evaluation of the present currency situation. In the first two decades after World War II, American capital flowed into foreign countries without there being any evidence of capital imports worth speaking of. Only after the capital markets of Europe had recovered their strength did European capital once more begin to flow into the United States. This movement might help to solve the difficult balance of payments problem.

2 Monetary, Fiscal, and Business Cycle Policies

1. *The Swiss Franc*

A sound currency is the first prerequisite for the rise of a financial center. The Swiss franc was created, on the French pattern, after the foundation of the Swiss Confederation in the middle of the nineteenth century. Up to that time there was a confused miscellany of currencies; indeed, nearly all cantons and many towns had coined their own money. The newly created Swiss franc was a currency based on silver. The subsidiary and silver coins issued in those days, from 1 rappen to 5 francs, are still in use, except that in 1931 the diameter and silver content of the 5-franc coin was reduced. Quite recently, however, the rising price of silver induced the Federal Government to switch from silver coins to coins of copper and nickel. At first strictly a silver currency, the Swiss franc in the eighteen-seventies became a bimetallic currency, based on both silver and gold. After dissolution of the Latin Monetary Union, a full-fledged gold standard was adopted by the Currency Act of 1930. With the devaluation of the Swiss franc in the year 1936, the obligation of the National Bank to redeem bank notes in gold was suspended. To ratify this change, a constitutional amendment, abolishing redeemability, was submitted to popular vote in 1948. It was rejected by a sizable majority. In 1951 to people were asked to cast their votes on another constitutional amendment under which the obligation to redeem notes in gold could be suspended only in times of war or troubled currency conditions. This was accepted at the polls. Now since, with a look at the world as a whole, we may well speak of troubled currency conditions even today, redeemability remains suspended. It would, in fact, be impossible for any one country to reintroduce a gold standard with actual circulation of gold coins, for these coins would flow across the frontier and become a disturbing factor in the world currency system. Given the present price of gold, they would soon disappear in hoardings anyway. Thus, whereas in point of form the Swiss currency system is still a gold coin standard, in point of fact we must speak of a gold bullion standard, with gold being kept in the bank of issue as cover for the note circulation and for the purpose of meeting difficulties in balance of payment situations, but without the bank being obligated to redeem the notes in gold. In Article 2 of the Monetary Act of December 17, 1952, the gold content of the Swiss franc was set at 0.20322... g of fine gold. The amended Monetary Act provided, moreover, for the issue of gold coins of 25 and 50 francs; they were coined, but have never shown up in circulation.

The fact that the gold content of the Swiss franc is anchored in law, means that its par value can be raised or reduced only by a change in law, that is, by action of the legislature. In the case of the dollar the legal situation is similar. When the Monetary Act was amended at the beginning of the fifties, the legislature was well aware of this situation. But it was deemed best once more to fix the parity by law in order to make parity changes as difficult as possible. (However, late in 1970 the parliamentary bodies did grant the Federal Government the authority to change the parity by its own action.) At the end of 1968 the circulation of Swiss bank notes was covered by gold at a rate of 94%. The Swiss franc has thus the highest gold coverage of any currency. Among the 12 most important industrial countries,[10] the Netherlands, with a gold coverage of 69%, take second place; Austria with 57% is third; then comes the German Federal Republic with 56%. The United States ranks ninth on this list. Even if, in addition to gold, foreign exchange is included in computing the coverage, we find the Swiss franc on top with 141%, followed by the Austrian schilling with 109% and the German mark with 104%. The two key currencies, the dollar and the pound sterling, take ninth and tenth place in this count. Since currency reserves now stand in only a loose relationship to the volume of note circulation and serve primarily to bridge balance of payments difficulties, their volume is frequently related to the volume of commodity imports. In Switzerland, 87% of the imports are covered by currency reserves. Even by this criterion, Switzerland

[10] United States, Canada, Great Britain, France, Germany, Italy, Belgium, Netherlands, Sweden, Austria, Japan, Switzerland.

ranks first, despite the huge volume of her imports; next comes Austria with 50%, followed by Italy, the German Federal Republic, and the United States. In the three last-named countries, about 40% of the imports are covered by currency reserves. Sweden and Great Britain, with about 13% each, rank far below by this calculation. On the liabilities side, even if accounts payable (demand deposits of the economy and the Federal Government) are added to notes in circulation, the coverage in Switzerland is 91%. It rises to 100% if we include on the assets side foreign Treasury Bonds in Swiss franc and deposits with foreign central banks that are not exposed to exchange rate fluctuations.

Confidence in a currency, however, also depends very much on the stability of the exchange rate. International comparison reveals that since the end of World War I, the French franc was devalued 14 times. The German currency was completely ruined in the first World War and was placed on a new basis in 1923. In 1948 there was another currency reform by which the former reichsmark was converted into deutschmark, 10:1 being the rate of conversion. Another downward revaluation occurred in the general devaluation wave of 1949. In 1961 came an upward revaluation by 5%, and in 1969 another one by 9.3%. Despite its checkered history the German currency today enjoys a good reputation because in the last few years the balances of payment were active and the currency reserves rose appreciably. The Italian lira has undergone six devaluations since the first World War and the Belgian franc eight; the Dutch guilder has experienced three devaluations and one appreciation, and the pound sterling six devaluations. Austria, after a conversion in 1925, has devalued her currency five times, Sweden and Canada have had three devaluations and one appreciation; the exchange value of the Canadian currency exhibited some flexibility over twelve years. The American dollar and the Swiss franc are the only currencies that were devalued only once, in the years 1934 and 1936, respectively. Since the Swiss franc has been devalued less than the dollar, it has experienced an appreciation relative to that currency, whereas all other currencies have, on balance, been depreciated in relation to the dollar.

However, the soundness of a currency also depends on its internal purchasing power. Typically, devaluations become necessary after prices in a country have risen at a higher rate than prices abroad. Until the year 1961, price inflation in Switzerland kept within tolerable bounds. Between 1953 and 1961 the average annual rate of inflation was not even quite 1%. Later, however, the boom years caused prices to rise at almost 4% in the annual average. Switzerland thus lost her privileged position in this respect. Setting the price levels of 1953 at 100, the cost of living index in Switzerland at the end of 1968 was 143 compared with 133 in the United States, 138 in the German Federal Republic, and 137 in Canada. In Britain, France, Italy and Sweden, the rate of inflation was higher.

Inflation rates of 4% are in the long run intolerable for a country as dependent on exports as Switzerland. In 1968 the rate could be reduced to 2.2%.

Currencies enjoying a high reputation frequently grow into a role which may be characterized as that of reserve currency, or key currency, or trade currency, or reference currency. Before the first World War, the pound sterling was the leading currency. In the interwar period it was replaced in this role by the American dollar. The international standing of the Swiss franc led to repeated attempts to use the Swiss franc as a reserve currency. The temptation to do so was particularly strong when, after the Suez crisis, Egypt's accounts in London and New York were temporarily frozen. Attempts were made repeatedly to use the Swiss franc as a currency basis for international loans or trade transactions. The Swiss National Bank has always fought this use of the franc. Being a small country with an economic potential that is not particularly strong when measured in world proportions, Switzerland is not in a position to furnish an international currency. Attempts to set up currency reserves in Swiss francs would fail because of the narrow limits of the Swiss money market, if for no other reason. The use of the Swiss franc for international capital or trade transactions could, moreover, cause disturbances on the Swiss money and foreign exchange market.

2. Monetary Policy

It was not until the year 1907 that Switzerland got a central bank of issue. Before that year the cantonal banks, and some private banks, issued bank notes. A first attempt to give the Confederation the right to set rules about the issue and redemption of bank notes was rejected in 1872, but was accepted 1874 in the framework of the partial revision of the Federal Constitution. But it was not until October 18, 1891, that the Confederation was given the right to create a central bank of issue. A first Federal bill, under which the bank of issue would have been organized as a government agency, failed in the plebiscite of 1897. A later attempt reached the goal: the Act of October 6, 1905, ratified the establishment of a bank of issue. By this Act, the Swiss National Bank was established as an independent joint-stock company. Slightly more than one half of the shares were held by the cantons and the cantonal banks; the rest was in the hands of private individuals. As an earlier draft of the bill had failed of acceptance because the question of the headquarters could not be settled, it was decided that the National Bank was to have two headquarters, one in Bern and one in Zurich. The cantons were to receive a portion of the National Bank's net profits, the portion to be determined on a per head of population basis. The dividend was limited to 6%.

In Switzerland there are relatively narrow limits to what the Bank of Issue can achieve by its policy. The Bank has at its disposal only an inconspicuous box of policy tools; these, moreover, are not too effective, given the structure of the Swiss money market. By setting rates of discount, or conditions of credit on securities, the Bank can accomplish little. The portfolio of bills of exchange amounted to 107 million francs in mid-March 1969. Credit on securities stood at 53 million francs at the same time. So the effect of changes in the rate of discount is largely psychological. It is true that some discount rates set by the banks usually follow the rate of the National Bank immediately. In the first few years after the foundation of the National Bank, changes in the rate of discount were still relatively frequent. From 1936 to 1956, however, the rate stood unchanged at 1½%. It was not until 1957 that an active discount policy was resumed, and even then great restraint was exercised. Although the National Bank Act was revised in 1953 to take account of the change in the legal situation since 1936, all that the revised Act provided was a minor widening of the scope of the open-market policy. The National Bank was authorized to purchase securities with terms up to three years. But the open-market policy could not become very effective, for the bank lacked an adequate portfolio of securities. In the last few years the Bank has resorted to the expedient of selling certain government bonds on the market on which it, the bank itself, has to pay interest. Such bonds are entered on the liabilities side of the Bank's balance sheet as long-term debts and amount to 375 million francs. So far the National Bank has lacked the instrument of minimum reserve requirements. However, according to the Bank Act, the National Bank has a say in the fixing of interest rates on demand deposits with the commercial banks. Capital exports in the form of public loans, or of bank credits exceeding 10 million francs and having a term of more than two years, are likewise subject to approval by the National Bank.

The inadequacy of its box of policy tools induced the National Bank to seek the cooperation of the commercial banks. As a rule this was done in the form of so-called gentlemen's agreements. In the interwar period one such agreement by which the banks undertook to consult the National Bank on capital exports was already in existence. This rule was later incorporated into the Bank Act. In the postwar period such agreements were concluded several times, for instance, about loans mortgaged on real estate, and about the voluntary keeping of minimum reserves. Starting in 1960 when large amounts of money were flowing into Switzerland, a gentlemen's agreement was concluded with the banks with a view to holding off such money. From then on, new foreign funds could be accepted in the country for only a specified time and no interest could be paid on them. Following the appreciation of the deutschmark and the Dutch guilder in the spring of 1961, the Swiss market was deluged by foreign money, whereupon roughly 1 billion francs were diverted, in agreement with the banks, to a special blocked account with the National Bank. As the economic uprising at the beginning of the sixties threatened to assume dangerous forms, the National Bank in the spring of 1962 concluded an agreement with the banks about restrictions to be imposed on bank credits. This novel type of intervention seemed necessary because credits granted by the banks in the years 1960-61 had grown to extraordinary proportions. The measures that had been adopted earlier to hold off money from abroad were continued. It turned out, however, that the boom could not be kept sufficiently in check by these voluntary measures. So the Federal Council in the spring of 1964 saw fit to propose, in urgent Federal resolutions, measures that could put a damper on the boom. By the so-called "Credit Resolution," bank credits were, in fact, placed under control.

The experience of the sixties showed definitely that the policy tools available to the National Bank were inadequate, and so the Federal Council assigned to the directorate of the bank the job of preparing an amendment to the National Bank Act. In the spring of 1969 a draft bill was sent to the National Assembly. It provided for the adoption of minimum reserve requirements, the control of the issue of bank notes, and the restriction of bank credit in certain exceptional situations. Also, the scope of open-market policy was to be widened by the reform. Government regulation in the field of monetary policy always encounters strong opposition in Switzerland; this had been clearly seen already when the National Bank was being established. Not surprisingly, then, the Commission set up by the National Council, while accepting the draft bill as a basis for action, decided in its deliberations during the summer of 1969 to try once more to achieve the desired control by way of an agreement between the Association of Swiss Banks and the Swiss National Bank.

In due course such an agreement was, in fact, concluded. In it the banks undertook to set up minimum reserves for additional credits granted or to restrict their granting of credits directly should the National Bank suggest one or the other of these courses. In case the contracting parties should not reach an understanding, the National Bank's Committee on Banking would make the decision. Sanctions could be imposed on banks that did not fulfill their obligations.

On the basis of this agreement, it was ruled late in the summer of 1969 that new (additional) credits by the banks would be limited to 9% or in exceptional cases to 11.5%. The purpose was to keep the boom within tolerable limits. Control of the issue of bonds was not included in the agreement because it had been incorporated in an earlier convention.

Since in this way the three most important measures provided for in the new National Bank Act had been put into effect on a contractual basis, the National Assembly decided not to take any further action with respect to the draft bill of the Federal Council.

The attempt to organize the policy tools of the bank of issue by agreement rather than by law was in conformity with the type of cooperation practiced even before between the commercial banks and the National Bank. What we have here is a specifically Swiss solution such as is conceivable only in a small country in which a close personal contact between the central bank and the commercial banks can be maintained. Whereas the experiment makes heavy demands on the banks, it is not doomed in advance to failure. This is all the more true as the banks are well aware that in case of failure, regulation by law will eventually follow.

Switzerland is not a member of the International Monetary Fund (IMF) or of the World Bank. There is a special story behind this fact. After the end of World War II, insurmountable obstacles were blocking the way to Swiss membership in the Monetary Fund. Article VIII of the Fund Agreement states that no member country may put into effect any foreign exchange regulations that would hamper foreign trade. It is true that Article XIV relieves all countries having to struggle with foreign exchange difficulties of this obligation. But Switzerland could not have invoked this article at the end of the war, for she had a convertible currency whereas all her European trade partners had exchange control. By concluding clearing agreements Switzerland endeavored to tie her imports to her exports, which was not reconcilable with Article VIII of the Fund Agreement. So Switzerland had to keep out of the Bretton Woods Institutes.

Now it is true that in the meantime all of the more important countries had switched to convertibility, and had accepted the obligations of Article VIII. The biggest obstacle was thus out of the way. A few other difficulties remained, however. The members of the Monetary Fund were obligated to keep their currencies at parity levels, with permitted deviations of only 1% upward or downward. The parity of the Swiss franc in terms of the dollar is 4.37. The upper intervention point was 4.2850 in the postwar period. From the spring 1961 to spring 1968, it was 4.3150, and since then, it has been 4.2950. The highest selling rate attained so far was 4.35. Thus the Swiss franc is keeping steadily above its parity level of 4.37, the recent upper intervention point lying 1¾% above par. If Switzerland were to join the International Monetary Fund, the upper intervention point would have to be changed from 4.2950 to the point corresponding to a 1% deviation from parity, that is, to 4.33. The narrow deviation limits prescribed by the International Monetary Fund would thus have the effect of restraining somewhat more sharply than has so far been the case the tendency of the franc to deviate from parity in the upward direction. As a result the actual average value of the franc as measured by the dollar would probably stay somewhat lower than it would in the absence of the narrow deviation limits set by the Monetary Fund.

The question of whether to join the Monetary Fund has been pondered repeatedly. Against joining up there is the consideration that Swiss monetary policy would have to sacrifice part of its autonomy. Considerations of solidarity speak for joining up. It has frequently been argued that drawings by the Fund on Switzerland might lead to the creation of additional Swiss francs and thus might have an inflationary effect. But on closer examination this argument seems hardly justified. A country that applies for credit with the Monetary Fund will wish to convert the Swiss francs placed at its disposal into dollars which have the standing of an international means of payment. If the conversion is effected at the Swiss National Bank, it does not entail any creation of additional money. Only the composition of the currency reserves will eventually change. Gold and foreign exchange will be replaced by balances with the Monetary Fund and later probably also by special drawing rights. This could in a certain degree restrict the National Bank's freedom of movement.

Although not a member of the Monetary Fund, Switzerland follows the Fund's guidance to a large extent. Dr. Jacobsson once told the author, "If all my members obeyed the rules of the Fund as conscientiously as Switzerland does, I should have far fewer worries."

However, a country such as Switzerland, which in the course of the years has grown into the role of an international financial center, cannot decline cooperation in the field of financial and monetary policy. And, in fact, Switzerland maintains good relations with the institutes of Bretton Woods. She has opened her capital market to the World Bank. From the end of the war until 1968, there were 14 loans, amounting to more than 900 million francs, issued. Moreover, the Confederation has repeatedly granted credits, 300 million francs in all, to the World Bank. To International Development Association (IDA), an institute affiliated with the World Bank, an interest-free loan of 52 million francs was granted.

When it turned out in 1961 that the International Monetary Fund was not strong enough to give effective assistance to key currency countries such as Great Britain or the United States, the so-called "General Agreements to Borrow" were concluded. In these agreements the ten strongest industrial countries undertook to extend to the Monetary Fund, if necessary, credits up to 6 million dollars. This seemed to open up an opportunity for Swiss cooperation. In principle Switzerland declared her willingness to participate in such a supporting credit action. There was, however, the difficulty that the International Monetary Fund could go into debt only in the currencies of its members. Hence, in the framework of the "General Agreements to Borrow," a credit to the Fund in Swiss francs was out of the question. A solution was eventually found in the following arrangement: In case use was made of the credit facilities provided by the "General Agreements," the International Monetary Fund could ask Switzerland to grant a "parallel credit" directly to the country that applied for help by the Fund. In such a case a so-called "Implementing Agreement" would be concluded between Switzerland and the country in question. The National Assembly has given its consent to this policy and has authorized the Federal Council by Resolution of October 4, 1963, to guarantee to the Swiss National Bank up to 865 million Swiss francs (200 million dollars) for operations of this kind.

3. Fiscal Policy

To cover the costs of mobilization during the second World War, the Federal Government found itself under the necessity of introducing a sales tax, heretofore unknown in Switzerland, and of widening substantially the scope of the Federal tax on income and property which had been introduced in the first World War and continued during the interwar period, with only small interruptions, as the so-called "crisis levy." A property tax, called "defense levy" (Wehropfer) was put into effect twice. In 1944 a tax levied at the source of property incomes, the so-called "accounting tax" (Verrechnungssteuer) was introduced. All these taxes were based on wartime powers of the Federal Council, which means that they had no constitutional basis.

In the postwar era it was evident that the Confederation would have to rely on the revenue from these taxes (except the defense levy) even in the future. So the problem was to secure constitutional legal grounds for them. This was a difficult task. In conservative bourgeois quarters the view was widespread that the sources of taxation should be distributed between the Confederation and the cantons, leaving the direct taxes to the cantons and allotting the indirect taxes to the Confederation. The people were also under the illusion that the Federal expenditures, which during the war had risen to about 2½ billion francs, could again be reduced to roughly 1.3 billion francs. In a first move, which led to lengthy parliamentary debates, the conservative thesis eventually won. But the proposed bill ran into strong opposition from the Left, and so it failed in the plebiscite. In a second move maintenance of the defense levy as well as the sales tax and the accounting tax was contemplated, but the Federal Council deemed it necessary to increase slightly the progression in the defense levy in order to offset the loss of revenue from the property tax, which was being abolished. This encountered opposition from bourgeois quarters, with the result that in 1952 this project, too, was rejected by popular vote. It took a third move to achieve success in 1958, and even then success came only because time limits had been set to the new taxes. One extension, with some minor amendments, was ratified by plebiscite without any major opposition.

The present state of affairs is scheduled to continue until 1974. The Federal

Council thinks, however, that the existing sources of tax revenue are no longer adequate to finance the mounting Federal expenditures, especially in the fields of research and education. This is believed to be all the more true as Federal revenues from tariffs have declined with the progress of European economic integration and as a result of the "Kennedy Round."

In the postwar era the government found it necessary to place expenditures under strict control and to revise superseded concepts. This was necessary because in the postwar period the sources of Federal revenue lacked a constitutional basis, and it was recognized that a plebiscite on maintenance of the taxes introduced in wartime could succeed only if public opinion was convinced that the government was economy-minded. So, among other things, all subsidies aimed at lowering the costs of living were abolished; but new tasks were waiting. Old-age and survivors insurance was introduced in 1949. The conflict between East and West necessitated new efforts in national defense. At the beginning of the fifties an armament program was carried through, although the Legislature would not have been willing to open up special financial sources for this program. The development of aviation made it necessary to develop the airports. Yet up to 1956 it proved feasible to keep Federal expenditures within the order of magnitude of 2 billion francs. In the years 1951-52 deficits arose amounting to 29 and 211 million francs, respectively. Subsequently, however, the rising revenues kept pace with the expenditures, although these rose by leaps and bounds from 1957 on, and in 1968 exceeded the 6-billion mark.

The development of the Federal revenues and expenditures can be seen on Table 1 below.

Thanks to the postwar surpluses, which at times were substantial, the Federal public debt, which by the end of the war had grown to 8.7 billion, could again be reduced to 5 billion. The deficit, which at the end of the war amounted to 8.4 billion francs, could even be lowered to 2.8 billion by the end of 1968. The difference is explained by the fact that the surpluses of the Federal accounts are only in part being used for the repayment of public debts. For reasons of business-cycle policy it was deemed advisable to channel part of the surpluses into short-term investments abroad. At first the funds were invested on the American money market on a short-term basis. Later U.S. Treasury bonds in Swiss francs (the so-called "Roosa bonds") were found to be the most suitable investment. At the end of 1968 the Swiss Federal Government owned such bonds in the amount of 480 million francs. Some funds were also being invested in the Bank for International Settlements and the World Bank. These investments reached 383 million francs at the close of 1968. There were, moreover, long-term credits to foreign government-owned railroads and to the German steel industry, and a residual credit balance from that "clearing billion" the origin of which we have already discussed.

40

Table 1. Closing Accounts of the Federal Government 1946 to 1968

	Millions of francs		
	Expen- diture	Reve- nues	Surplus
1946	2212.9	2411.3	198.4
1947	1946.7	2208.9	262.2
1948	1946.7	2239.3	292.6
1949	1581.4	1639.7	58.3
1950	1637.0	1973.7	336.7
1951	1786.5	1757.3	− 29.2
1952	2161.5	1949.9	−211.6
1953	1884.0	1974.8	90.8
1954	1959.2	2320.2	361.0
1955	1948.7	2245.3	296.6
1956	1963.6	2610.6	647.0
1957	2238.2	2440.3	202.1
1958	2643.2	2826.2	183.0
1959	2482.4	2722.7	240.3
1960	2601.1	3316.1	715.0
1961	3267.1	3406.0	138.9
1962	3684.2	4116.6	432.4
1963	4082.9	4209.3	126.4
1964	4856.6	5276.7	420.1
1965	4920.3	4951.7	31.4
1966	5682.9	5687.6	4.7
1967	5873.8	5717.8	−156.0
1968	6446.7	6603.5	156.8
1969	7080.8	7108.4	27.6

The favorable development of the Federal budget helped greatly in restraining the inflationary forces that almost unavoidably made their appearance in an economy with full employment. The policy aimed at keeping these forces in check was further supported by the growth of the equalization fund of the old-age and survivors insurance, which in the first few years had the effect of an arrangement for compulsory saving. The fund increased from 1948 to 1963 by slightly more than 400 million francs in the annual average. Since then the growth has slowed down markedly, owing to the rise of payments to insured persons. In 1956 and 1960, the combined surplus of the Government and the OASI exceeded the billion mark, and until 1964 it kept within the order of magnitude of 600 million francs. This development may have contributed to the fact that on the average the cost of living for the years 1953 to 1961 rose less than 1% per year. With the decrease of these surpluses since 1962, in a period

At the end of 1968 the foreign claims of the Federal Government were as follows:

	Million Swiss francs
Short-term investments in USA (in sfcs)	480
World Bank and BIS	383
Long-term credits	940
Total	1803

when the economy became overstrained, the rate of inflation picked up, and it was not until 1968 that it slowed down again.

In the budget for the year 1969 about 1.9 billion out of the approximately 7 billion francs of total Federal spending represent expenditures for defense. Social policy takes about 1.2 billion. For road building, 920 million francs have been allocated; subsidies to agriculture reach an order of magnitude of 880 million francs. Finally, the cantons share in the Federal revenue to the tune of 375 million francs. Interest payment on the Federal debt takes 180 million.

Long before business was willing to publish consolidated balance sheets, the Federal Government drew up a balance sheet that included post, telegraph, and telephone, as well as the Swiss Federal railroads. The 1968 balance sheet compared with 1958 is shown in Table 2.

A comparison of the two balance sheets reveals that debt repayment has not proceeded as satisfactorily as it might appear at first glance. Although the Federal Government itself has reduced its public debt from 6,790 to 5,779 million in the course of the last decade, the debt incurred by post, telegraph, and telephone through postal checking accounts has risen from 2,316 to 5,786 million. Moreover the balance sheets reveal the extent to which the postal administration has financed its investments by short-term money in the form of such checking accounts. In the years 1958 to 1968, it invested 4.8 billion, and in the same period its debt via postal checking accounts rose by 3.47 billion. And the consolidated balance sheet refutes the widespread belief that the Federal Government has no short-term debts worth speaking of. Through the post, telegraph and telephone, and postal checking accounts, the Government does have such debts and they add up to a substantial amount. Whereas the public debt of the Government was reduced by 1.3 billion during the decade 1958 to 1968, the indebtedness originating in postal checking accounts has risen in the same time span from 2.3 to 5.8 billion. It has thereby reached the level of the Government's own direct debts.

Even so, there is reason to be satisfied with the consolidated balance sheet of the Federal Government. The debt proper (owed to creditors outside the Federal

42

Table 2.

	1958		1968	
	Millions of francs			
Assets				
Plant, equipment, and administrative property				
Government	3,768		7,463	
Depreciation	1,357	2,411	2,448	5,015
PTT [a]	3,013		8,328	
Depreciation	1,431	1,582	3,642	4,686
SFR [a]	5,138		8,141	
Depreciation	2,382	2,756	3,760	4,381
Net plant, equipment, and administrative property		6,749		14,082
International payments agreements		34		7
Prepaid expenses (of which National road 2061)		–		2,119
Deficit				
Government	6,680		2,766	
Net property PTT	98		103	
Net property SFR	66	6,516	99	2,564
Total		13,299		18,772
Liabilities				
Debts				
Government	6,790		5,779	
PTT	2,316		5,786	
SFR	624	9,730	324	11,889
Internal accounting adjustments				
Government	215		155	
PTT	–90		14	
SFR	36	161	–	169
Reserves and Special Funds				
Government	3,030		5,325	
PTT	26		69	
SFR	352	3,408	1,320	6,714
Total		13,299		18,772

[a] PTT stands for post, telegraph, and telephone, SFR stands for Swiss Federal Railroads.

establishment) amounts to 11.9 billion francs, of which 6.1 billion are direct debts of the Government and the Swiss Federal Railroads, and 5.8 billion originate in postal checking accounts. There are also internal liabilities such as reserves and special funds. On the assets side we have:

	Millions of francs
Liquid assets of the government	572
Claims and fixed assets	1,938
Loans	1,372
Financial interests	157
Inventories	355
Total	4,394

To this may be added certain claims against foreign state railroads. These claims were entered on the accounts of the Swiss Federal Railroads; they amount to 455 million francs.

The Government's plant—administrative buildings in and outside the country, storage facilities for weapons, military work shops, etc.—is valued 3 billion at cost, and has been written down to 0.9 billion. The plant of the Federal railroads is valued 4.4 billion after depreciation of 3.76 billion; the plant of the post, telegraph, and telephone is entered at 4.7 billion after depreciation of 3.6 billion. Besides these true assets, we have on the assets side prepaid expenses for national road building in the amount of 2061 million francs. Part of the high cost of national road building has been accounted for in this way; so this item does not represent a true asset. The debts owed to creditors outside the Federal establishment, amounting to 11.9 billion, are covered by assets of 14.1 billion. Adding on the liabilities side the reserves and on the asset side the prepaid expenses for road building, a deficit of 2.56 billion francs results, as compared with 6.5 billion francs in 1968.

To be able to appraise the balance sheet position it is also necessary to look at the performances in the field of social assistance. In some otherwise well-balanced government budgets, these performances are a heavy burden. The Swiss old-age and survivors insurance has a fund of 7.3 billion, the Swiss Institute for Accident Insurance has one amounting to 2.5 billion. These funds, totaling roughly 10 billion, have been invested almost exclusively in assets other than securities issued by the Federal Government. Thus, in the portfolio of the old-age and survivors insurance, government securities amount to only 0.2 billion. Even a critical observer will have to conclude that the financial situation of the Federal Government, including government enterprises and social accounts, is sound.

In appraising the state of the Federal finances, account must be taken of the fact that Switzerland never had an inflation that completely decimated the public debt, as was the case in neighboring countries. Nor can the healthy condition of the Federal finances be fully explained by the policy of neutrality. Before and during the second World War, Switzerland spent more for defense purposes per head of the population than any other continental European country except the Third Reich. It would lead too far afield to investigate in detail the causes of the healthy condition of the Federal finances. But two factors, which are usually overlooked, should be mentioned.

Remembering the coal shortage that had existed during the first World War, the Federal railroads in the interwar period pushed ahead with the electrification of the whole railway network. As a result railway traffic could be maintained during World War II, in contrast to what had happened in World War I. Since much of the cost of the electrification could be written off, the Federal railroads in the postwar era were able to operate for two decades without incurring any deficit, and for a few years they were even in a position to pay interest on the capital that had been allotted to them.

The PTT started automation of telephones early. The work was finished in a period when other countries were just beginning to tackle the project. Thus the telephone plants could meet the increased demand without adding to their personnel. The PTT were able to bear the deficits of the letter and parcel post service, and, moreover, to make periodic refunds to the Federal Government, amounting to 70 million francs per year in most cases.

On the future development of the Federal accounts, rather bleak forecasts have repeatedly been put forward. Thus an opinion dating from 1966 expected that Federal expenditures would rise more rapidly than revenues, resulting in a deficit of 1.8 billion francs in 1973. The medium-term financial planning of the administration reached similar conclusions. These pessimistic forecasts can be explained by the fact that in the years 1964 to 1966 Federal spending rose steeply as new tasks were taken up in the fields of road building and social security, whereas revenues declined between 1964 and 1967 as a result of the tariff reductions in the framework of the European Free Trade Association (EFTA). A continuation of these trends would indeed have led to large deficits. In the year 1967 the financial accounts, for the first time since 1952, closed with a deficit, amounting to 156 million francs. In 1968 the Federal revenues regained their former rate of growth, whereas the trend of expenditures flattened out somewhat. The result was that the year closed with a revenue surplus of 157 million francs. Assuming steadily prosperous business conditions, one can count on an annual increase in revenues of 450 to 500 million francs. With careful planning of expenditures it should therefore be possible even in the future to keep the Federal budget balanced.

The Federal budget represents only a part of the public finances of the Confederation. In 1966 total Federal expenditures of 5.7 billion were accompanied by expenditures of 6.4 billion by the cantons and 4.5 billion by the communities. The total public spending that resulted after elimination of all double counting, was roughly 14 billion francs—22% of the gross national product for the same year. Of the direct income and property taxes, which totaled 6,390 million francs, 1,349 went to the Federal Government, 2,535 million to the cantons, and 2,506 million to the communitites. Of the consumption taxes, 3,494 million were received by the Federal Government, 287 million by the cantons, and 30 million by the communities. Clearly, then, the bulk of the indirect taxes flows to the Federal Government, whereas the bulk of the direct taxes goes to the cantons, although it is true that the Federal Government has made quite substantial inroads into tax revenue that was originally earmarked for the cantons.

4. Business Cycle Policy

Under the impression of what had been experienced in the world economic crisis, a Swiss business cycle policy evolved for the first time immediately before and after the second World War. The aim was to avoid in the future the volume of unemployment that had existed in the thirties. In the critical year 1940, when it seemed advisable to strengthen the people's stamina, the President of the Confederation promised the Swiss people that after the end of the war, employment opportunities would be created, whatever the cost. A commission for studying the question was set up, and, pursuant to its recommendations, a delegate was appointed with the assignment to work on the problems connected with the creation of job opportunities. Since it was difficult to place tax policy into the service of an active business cycle policy, the main emphasis was on a policy of public works. The plan was to counteract a threatening crisis by a countercyclical spending policy. The Federal Government, the cantons, and the communities, were asked to plan their orders for construction well in advance so as to be able to activate them without delay in times of crisis. A major public works program was developed, and it contributed in no small degree to strenghthening the stamina of the people and the army during the difficult war years.

As we have seen, it was found possible in the postwar years, through credits granted in the framework of existing trade and payment agreements, to expand the export business so greatly that a shortage of manpower soon made itself felt despite the restraint displayed by the public agencies in giving new orders to business. Foreign workers had to be employed to meet the demand; their number increased from year to year, reaching a peak of 700,000 in the summer of 1964. The proportion of foreigners in the economically active Swiss population was then almost one third and this gave rise to some concern from the economic as well as the political point of view; so the Federal Council found it advisable to check the inflow of foreign labor after 1964.

As a result of Switzerland becoming flooded with foreign labor, considerable investments were necessary to provide working places, dwelling, and equipment. Despite a volume of residential construction never attained before—50,000 to 55,000 dwelling units per year—it was only around 1967 that supply and demand on the market for residential construction could be approximately balanced. In the hospitals a shortage of beds soon developed, and as the families of the foreign workers immigrated to join them, new school buildings had to be added. The workers from abroad sent a considerable portion of their wages to their families in the home countries, thereby causing a shrinkage, by 1.5 to 1.6 billion francs in the net earnings remaining in the country. Thus the foreign workers, while contributing to consumption and investment, did not make an adequate contribution to capital formation by saving. It was only due to the high volume of the savings performed by the Swiss population that an excessive disproportion between capital formation and investment could be avoided. Even so, rates of interest did go up.

Construction activity increased from year to year. The volume of construction, which had been 3.8 billion in 1955, rose to 10 billion in 1963, and settled down in the following years at a level of between 11 and 12 billion. In view of this steep upward movement, and following a suggestion by the Federal Council, building boards (Baugremien), which were to examine the urgency of building projects, were set up in the cantons. This measure was taken simultaneously with the voluntary restriction of credit granting. But when it turned out in the two following years that the voluntary restraints were of no avail, the Federal Council, with a view to dampening the boom, passed two resolutions, known as the "building resolution" (Baubeschluss) and the "credit resolution" (Kreditbeschluss). The latter has already been mentioned in another connection. In the framework of the building resolution, construction of certain luxury buildings was made dependent on permits. For legal reasons these so-called "boom-dampening resolutions" (Konjunkturdaempfungsbeschluesse) could be put into effect for only one year. A plebiscite was required for an extension. Although the resolutions were by no means popular, in the spring of 1965 the people agreed to an extension for one more year. The slackening of the boom made it possible for the Federal Council to let the building resolution expire at the end of 1966. The rules of the credit resolution were gradually relaxed during the year 1967. Eventually the whole resolution was dropped before the end of the term originally contemplated.

The business cycle policy of the Swiss authorities encountered much criticism in the homeland. Government intervention to influence cyclical movements of the economy are rarely popular, especially when the purpose is to dampen an excessive boom. If in boom times the government refrains from taking restrictive measures and a recession sets in later, the government will be blamed for not having intervened in time. If it does adopt measures aimed at keeping the boom in check, it must expect to be blamed by those who were adversely affected by these measures.

The objective of modern business cycle policy is to secure full employment with prices as stable as possible and the balance of payments in equilibrium. This combination is sometimes referred to as a "magic triangle" because it is so difficult to achieve the three objectives at the same time. In order to arrive at a fair appraisal it is useful to compare the business cycle policies of the most important countries with one another. This has been attempted in the diagrams shown on pages 50-51. They show the development of employment as indicated by the statistics of unemployment, of the cost of living, and of the currency reserves. Taking Switzerland and the countries of the so-called "Club of Ten"except Japan, the indices of the cost of living, at mid-1969, setting 1953 = 100, were as follows.

	Consumer price index Mid-1969 (1953 = 100)
United States	137.5
Canada	141
Western Germany	141.7
Belgium	142.2
Switzerland	145.4
Italy	162.5
Great Britain	170
Sweden	172.8
Netherlands	175.8
France	190

Despite an acceleration of the rising trend of prices in the last few years, the United States still exhibits the smallest rate of inflation. We find Canada and three European countries with indices between 141 and 145, Western Germany ranking first. Italy and Great Britain follow at some distance. From the viewpoint of price stability, we have to eliminate France, the Netherlands, and Sweden from the contest in the inner circle. These countries have achieved

48

approximately full employment since 1953, but only by sacrificing price stability.

Turning to the criterion of equilibrium in the balance of payments, it is evident that Great Britain, which has been in a serious balance of payments crisis since 1964, is outside the contest. Nor can the United States, whose balance of payments was in the red except for the years 1957 and 1968, enter the contest in the inner ring, quite apart from the fact that the United States had recessions in 1954, 1958, and 1961. Canada, Italy, and France, likewise have had critical balance of payments situations since 1953. France found it necessary to devalue her currency in 1958 and 1969, while Italy was able to weather successfully a balance of payments crisis at the beginning of the sixties. But then Italy had a relatively high volume of unemployment during the whole period under observation; the number of unemployed never dropped below 500,000 and would probably have been higher still had not Italian workers found earning opportunities as "guest labor" in Germany, Switzerland, and elsewhere. Nor did Canada attain full employment; indeed, the number of unemployed since 1957 was for the most part above 400,000, in a population of about 18 million.

Hence, Western Germany, Belgium, and Switzerland are the countries most successful in handling the magic triangle. The three stand in the order just cited if price stability is regarded as the most important criterion. If the appraisal is based on the level of employment, then Switzerland comes out on top. From 1953 to 1960 the number of unemployed was always below 1 per mil of the population; since 1951 it has kept below 1,000, and since 1964, even below 300. In the Netherlands, unemployment in 1953, 1958, and 1967, rose above 80,000, that is, 6 per mil of population. In Belgium, too, unemployment never declined below 26,000, whereas Germany had full employment from 1960 to 1966, with a rate of unemployment under 3 per mil of the population most of the time. Only in 1967 did unemployment rise to 444,568 as a result of the credit restrictions introduced in that year.

Of particular interest is a comparison of the German and Swiss economic developments. Up to the year 1966 there was full employment in both countries, and both had to call in foreign labor. The cost of living index was hovering around 133 in Germany as well as in Switzerland. In both countries, the government and the central bank took restrictive measures. In Germany, where the absence of perfect equilibrium in the play of economic forces made itself felt more strongly, credit restrictions had to be applied more tightly, with the result that investment activity slowed down and the number of unemployed rose markedly, whereas in Switzerland unemployment stayed at the zero level. On the other hand the cost of living index rose 5 points in Switzerland and only 1 point in Germany, so that by the end of 1968 Germany had beaten Switzerland by 4 points. In order to overcome the 1966 recession more swiftly,

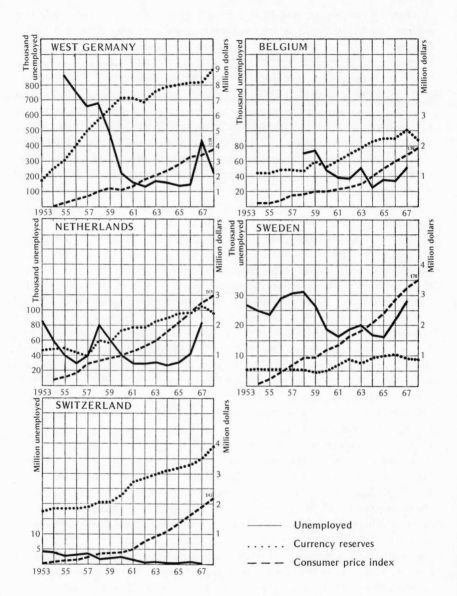

50

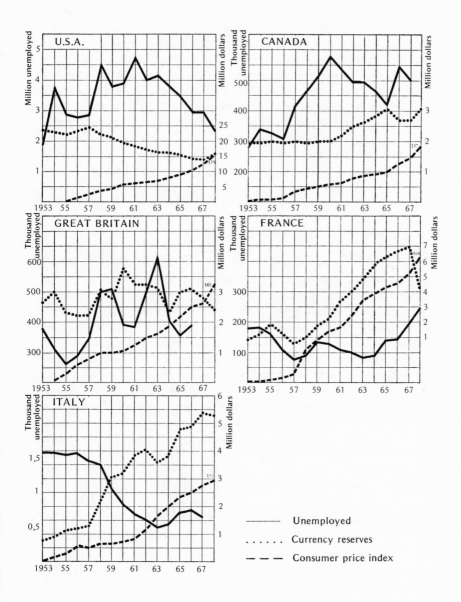

stimulating measures were again taken in 1967. In combination with a rebound of the world economy in the years 1968-69, they led to another boom. The somewhat too noisy discussion about an appreciation of the German mark (D-Mark) had repeatedly induced speculative inflows of short-term funds into Germany. At the end of September, 1969, this situation induced the coalition government, which was about to resign, to free the foreign exchange rate—a measure that so far had been resorted to in only quite extraordinary situations. Thus if we ask which country deserves the award for the best business cycle policy, the answer depends on whether we consider the level of employment or the stability of the level of prices as more important. In Germany, which had lived through two inflations since 1918, they were willing to accept the stabilization policy of the monetary authorities even at the price of 400,000 unemployed. In Switzerland the people would hardly have been willing to pay this price.

5. Cooperation between Central Banks

At the end of 1958 the monetary authorities of Britain, Germany, Italy, and France decided to terminate the European Payments Union and to make their currencies convertible. France, struggling with a deficit in her balance of payments and an inflated price level, thought she could not take this step without simultaneously devaluing the French franc. The Board of Managers of the Swiss National Bank asked themselves whether the step was not somewhat premature, for it seemed that not all currencies were as yet sufficiently consolidated to meet the requirements of convertibility. But it certainly was not for Switzerland to counsel restraint. After all, the Swiss franc was already convertible except for such restrictions as were necessary for performing payments transactions through the European Payments Union. In those days, the Swiss franc was the only European currency that could be converted into dollars without any restriction.

In the first one-and-a-half years the regime of convertibility worked without difficulty. In 1960, however, first signs of a crisis in confidence appeared in connection with the Congo crisis and the rising gold prices in October of that year. The huge deficits in the balance of payments of the United States during the years 1958 to 1960, and the impending presidential election, gave rise to certain doubts regarding the stability of the dollar. And the upward tendency in the price of gold was interpreted in many quarters as presaging a devaluation of the dollar. This led to uncertainties on the foreign exchange markets.

The large surplus in Western Germany's balance of payments induced the German government at the beginning of March, 1961, to raise the value of the

German mark by 5%. The Netherlands followed with a similar step. The financial world, which believed that this was the beginning of a general realignment of currencies, pondered which currencies were likely to be adjusted downward or upward. These quarters more or less expected a devaluation of the pound and an upward revaluation of the Swiss franc.

Management of the Swiss National Bank, in agreement with the Federal Council, held that a change in the parity of the Swiss franc was out of the question, all the ·more so because, as has already been pointed out, this would have required a change in the law. The management decided to defend the Swiss franc at an exchange rate of 4.3150 per dollar. On the Monday after the revaluation of the D-Mark those banks that were in the foreign exchange business were told that the dollar exchange rate of 4.3150 would be held under all circumstances and that for the time being and until further notice the banks could hold inflowing dollars under a guarantee by the National Bank. Within a few hours the Swiss banks had taken in 200 million dollars. Yet the dollar rate remained unchanged. This meant that, on the whole, the assault on the Swiss franc was repulsed. Toward the evening of that day one could already notice that some foreign banks were reorienting their operations accordingly.

So the "bullish" speculation against the Swiss franc had failed. But the attack against the pound was still in progress, and this caused another influx of some 100 million dollars by the end of the same week. The management of the National Bank had a difficult decision to make. Should they, in accordance with the practice followed so far, convert the accumulating dollars into gold, thereby taking the risk still "talked about" that the dollar might become even weaker? And could they look on without lifting a finger when the pound was running into difficulties caused by speculative transactions? Facing a simultaneous attack on two currencies, "bullish" in one direction and "bearish" in the other, a joint action by the two central banks suggested itself. The objective was to convince the financial world that there was no point in directing short-term funds from England to Switzerland if these funds were soon going to be redirected by the National Bank to the Bank of England. It was obvious that the cooperating central banks could hold their breath longer than the speculators. So the management of the Swiss National Bank decided to offer to the Bank of England an arrangement by which the funds that had flown into Switzerland would be placed at their disposal in the form of a dollar deposit or gold-sterling swap. The proposition was so unusual that in the ensuing talks there was at first uncertainty as to whether such a transaction was at all feasible from a legal viewpoint. But this question could soon be answered in the affirmative. Encouraged by the Swiss offer, the Bank of England contacted other central banks and these joined in the action. First the Swiss National Bank placed a deposit of 200 million dollars with the Bank of England. In the following weeks the plan of a gold-sterling swap was also tackled; it was carried out in four operations of 10 million pounds each. This first international action to support the pound reached the volume of 1.2 billion dollars, of which about one third originated with the Swiss National Bank. Such transactions were later called "Basel Agreements."

The first supporting action for the pound was performed without the United States. But the American monetary authorities watched it with a keen interest, and in numerous conversations the question was discussed as to how similar currency crises might be bridged in the future.

At that time the forward exchange market, which had been thrown completely out of gear by the events, gave rise to considerable concern. After the upward revaluation of the German mark, the customers of German industry demanded to be billed in their own currencies. This called for certain measures hedging against risks connected with foreign exchange rates, and these measures exerted pressure on the forward exchange rates of the two key currencies on the German market. In Switzerland forward dollars and pounds were at a discount that, at times, exceeded the interest on a three-months time deposit. This brought the short-term capital export to a standstill. So the German Federal Bank in cooperation with the Federal Reserve Bank of New York, which acted as an agent of the United States Treasury Department, began buying forward dollars against the deutschmark. And the Swiss National Bank succeeded in convincing the American monetary authorities that by supporting the forward rate of the dollar on the Swiss market, it would be possible to check the influx of short-term funds and in due course to get the export of capital moving again. And so since the Swiss National Bank had no legal authority to intervene on the forward exchange markets, purchases of forward dollars against Swiss francs were made in the summer of 1961 for the account of the American treasury.

Toward the end of the year forward exchange commitments of the United States Treasury Department amounted to more than 200 million Swiss francs. In Washington experts began wondering how the contracts in forward exchange could be settled at maturity. At that time no previous experience with interventions of this kind existed, and it was not yet known that once conditions would become normal again it would be relatively easy to liquidate the commitments. The American treasury felt it was very important for it to have Swiss francs available as a counterpart to its obligations on the forward exchange market. The Swiss were willing to lend the United States Treasury Swiss francs for, say, three months, and to accept a U.S. Treasury bond in return. At that time the Confederation possessed substantial liquid funds that were to be invested in interest-bearing foreign assets, a task in which the protection of exchange rates met with difficulties because of the described conditions on the forward exchange markets. But it was not yet clear whether it was legal for the

United States to incur a debt denominated in a foreign currency. This question had first to be clarified.

The legal experts of the United States Treasury went to work on the problem. It did not take them long to find an act, dating from the period after World War I, which authorized the United States to borrow in foreign currencies. The last credit transaction of this kind has been performed in 1922 when a loan in Spanish pesetas had been granted. On this legal basis, a first credit operation involving 100 million Swiss francs and a term of three months was effected. It was supplemented soon afterwards by a second transaction in the same amount. No sooner had the news of the transactions come into the open, than the Banca d'Italia let it be known in New York that it was willing to engage in a similar operation. Subsequently the United States issued bonds, with terms of one to one and a half years, that came to be known as "Roosa bonds," after R. V. Roosa, then Under-Secretary of the Treasury. The prolonged term had the advantage that such transactions could be entered in the United States balance of payments as capital inflow, which contributed to reducing the balance of payments deficit. However, these securities were given only to governments and to foreign central banks, and in the case of the latter, short-term redeemability was inserted. This had to be done because central banks may not, in general, hold longer-term securities.

In the winter of 1961-62 the question being studied was how swap transactions between central banks could be placed in the service of monetary cooperation. Out of the talks on the question grew the plan of a swap-net between the Federal Reserve System and the other central banks, with the objective of "hedging" the exchange rate for short-term dollar inflows to non-United States central banks. The final goal was to reduce as far as possible the scope of conversions of dollar balances into gold. Subsequently swap agreements were concluded on a stand-by basis between the Federal Reserve Bank of New York, which this time acted as an agent of the Federal Reserve System and quite a number of central banks. First, the Swiss National Bank concluded a swap agreement, involving 100 million dollars, with the New York Federal Reserve Bank. At the same time, a swap agreement was arranged between the New York Federal Reserve Bank and the Bank for International Settlements (BIS). The Swiss National Bank gave the Bank for International Settlements the binding assurance that it would provide this institute with the required francs against gold whenever the New York Federal Reserve Bank would draw on the swap, as indeed it repeatedly did afterwards. In time it turned out that the limits were inadequate and several raises followed. The swap facilities were utilized to a maximum extent at the end of 1967 when, in the aftermath of the devaluation of the pound, the Swiss banks supplied large amount of spot dollars to the National Bank. At that time the two swaps were utilized to the tune of 650 million dollars. In March, 1968, when it was decided to establish what has come to be known as the "two-tier" system of gold, there was reason to fear that this measure might have repercussions on the foreign exchange markets and the Euromarket. So the two swap lines were raised to $600 million each, but the ceiling did not have to be utilized in full. The New York Federal Reserve Bank was now in a position to draw 1.2 billion dollars equivalent in Swiss francs from the Swiss National Bank and the Bank for International Settlements.

The cooperation between the central banks was put to a severe test when in the autumn of 1964 the British pound once more underwent heavy pressure. The balance of payments exhibited a sizable deficit in that year. Even before the new elections, each of several friendly central banks, among them the Swiss National Bank, helped the Bank of England with 100 million dollars. As a result of the change in the Administration, the crisis of confidence became more intense, with the result that the newly formed Labor government was confronted with a difficult situation right from the start. The International Monetary Fund opened a credit of 1 billion dollars; this was possible only by making use, to the extent of 425 million dollars, of the "General Arrangement to Borrow." Referring to the agreement between Switzerland and the International Monetary Fund, an "Implementing Agreement" was concluded between Switzerland and Great Britain. It was utilized, paralleling the International Monetary Fund credit to the extent of 80 million dollars. However, despite a drastic raise in discount rates and backing by the International Monetary Fund, the crisis in confidence could not be overcome. So a central bank credit of 3 billion dollars became necessary. This had its psychological effect. The credit was utilized only for about one half of the credit line and in the spring of 1965 it was supplemented by another IMF credit amounting to 1.4 billion dollars. Even this credit could only be arranged by invoking the "General Arrangement to Borrow." Concurrently with the credit, Switzerland supplied to the Bank of England 40 million dollars in the framework of the implementing agreement and in the form of a franc-sterling swap. In the summer of 1966 another assistance action, partly through the Bank for International Settlements was arranged in order to replace the outflowing so-called sterling holdings. In the fall of 1966 the tables turned. Short-run funds streamed back to Great Britain. The Bank of England found itself placed in a position where it could repay the still outstanding central bank credits as well as part of the International Monetary Fund credit. This enabled the Monetary Fund to repay the credits that had been granted in the framework of the "General Agreement to Borrow." On this occasion the first parallel credit granted by the Swiss National Bank, which dated from the fall of 1964 and amounted to 80 million dollars equivalent, was also repaid. Then came another turn for the worse. In connection with the Near

East crisis, the Arab countries threatened to withdraw their balances in England, and the closing of the Suez Canal had unfavorable effects on the British balance of trade. Once more the pound underwent strong pressure, which eventually (November 18, 1967) induced the British government to devalue the pound by 14.3%. In the aftermath of the devaluation new credits were granted to the Bank of England, the Swiss National Bank participating with 75 million dollars.

The devaluation of the pound generated the most serious confidence crisis of the postwar era. Demand for gold reached the level of 3 billion dollars. Again Great Britain was the hardest hit, with the result that new supporting credits had to be opened to the Bank of England simultaneously, with the establishment of the two-tier system of gold in March, 1968.

Since it turned out in the course of the year 1968 that the sterling countries were striving to withdraw their balances from England in order to invest them elsewhere, a supporting action was once more brought, with the aim of offsetting the losses caused by these withdrawals. The term of this supporting credit, which was arranged through the Bank for International Settlements, was medium-long. In this way the total commitment of the Swiss National Bank once more reached 200 million dollars, for which amount the Federal Government, pursuant to a Federal Resolution of October 4, 1964, provided financial backing.

In the framework of the monetary cooperation, the Swiss National Bank in the years 1961 to 1968 granted currency credits totaling 14 billion francs, of which 1.7 billion were still outstanding in the spring of 1969. The credit lines on stand-by basis at that time amounted to about 1.2 million francs.

The swap arrangement with the New York Federal Reserve Bank has proved its worth in the last few years. Again and again there was a major influx of money into Switzerland, either because of unrest in international currency policy or because of a narrowing of the money market at home. In such cases the swap was activated by the New York Federal Reserve Bank. Thanks to the recurrent needs of the Federal Government and the Postal Administration for foreign exchange—needs that were being taken care of directly by the National Bank—it was possible as a rule to reduce much of the volume of the swaps. Things could not be completely balanced, however; the currency reserves of the Swiss National Bank were rising year after year. To facilitate the settlement of the swap obligations, the Swiss National Bank repeatedly took in so-called "Roosa bonds." By the summer of 1969 these holdings had grown to 1,851 million francs. Every now and then such operations were conducted through the Bank for International Settlements, which in the spring of 1969 was holding 1,115 million francs of these bonds. Taking account of the bonds in possession of the Federal Government and the Bank for International Settlements, American certificates of indebtedness in Swiss francs outstanding on September

Table 3.

	January 1968	March 1969	September 1969
	Millions of Dollars		
German Federal Bank	601.2	1125.7	1199.7
German banks	–	125.1	125.1
Swiss National Bank (including Federal Government and BIS)	362.9	726.8	744.7
Italy	124.8	225.6	125.4
Belgium	60.4	–	–
Austria	50.3	50.3	25.1
Total	1199.6	2253.5	2220.0

10, 1969, totaled 3,209 million francs, equivalent to 744.7 million dollars. On January 1, 1968, in March, 1969, and in September, 1969, the Roosa bonds issued by the United States were distributed among individual countries as shown in Table 3.

By the spring of 1969, the German Federal Bank, the Swiss National Bank, and the Bank for International Settlements had all greatly increased their holdings of Roosa bonds, whereas Belgium had made it a point to be fully reimbursed by that time. United States Treasury bonds denominated in foreign currencies were then supplied for the first time to German private banks. These bonds were, however, medium-term securities, with maturities slightly over four years. During the summer of 1969, Italy and Austria reduced their holdings by 100 and 25 million dollars, respectively.

In October, 1969, the swap network of the United States reached the level of 11 billion dollars. Fourteen countries and the Bank for International Settlements were involved. The credit lines are shown in Table 4.

By January, 1968, the United States had drawn upon their swap facilities to the tune of 1,775.8 million dollars. By the spring of 1969, the commitments were reduced to 40 million dollars in all. At that time the Swiss National Bank was the only creditor of the Federal Reserve System. By September, 1969, even this claim was settled. On the other hand, the United States in January, 1969, opened credits in the amount of 1,667.5 million dollars to her swap partners. Of these, 1,150 million dollars were granted to Great Britain, and 430 million to France. By the end of August, the amount outstanding could be reduced to 1,308.7 million. France settled her swap indebtedness in the second quarter, and Britain reduced hers to 975 million, whereas Belgium and the Netherlands

Table 4.

	Swap Network of U.S.A.
	Million dollars
Austria	200
Belgium	500
Canada	1,000
Denmark	200
Britain	2,000
France	1,000
Germany	1,000
Italy	1,000
Japan	1,000
Mexico	130
Netherlands	300
Norway	200
Sweden	250
Switzerland 600 ⎫	
⎬	1,200
BIS (Swiss francs) 600 ⎭	
BIS (other currencies)	1,000
Total	10,980

utilized their credit facilities to the extent of 224 and 109.7 million, respectively. The figures show the high degree to which balancing in either direction could be achieved through the swap system. And they show the active participation of Switzerland in the cooperation of central banks. It must not be overlooked, however, that the other countries were fulfilling their solidarity obligations via the International Monetary Fund. So the main importance of Switzerland's relatively high share in the American swap network and in the holdings of Roosa bonds, lay in providing some supplementary balancing.

3 The Structure of the
Swiss Financial Center

1. *The Banks*

(a) *In General*

The Swiss banking system is characterized by the extraordinary density of its network. At the end of 1968 the banking statistics listed 463 banks and 1146 rural loan associations; and there also were 47 private banks and 19 branches of foreign banks. These 1675 institutes had 4337 banking offices. Thus, given a population of about 6 million, there is, roughly, one banking office for every 1400 persons. The development in the postwar period may be illustrated by the figures in Table 5.

Table 5 shows that local banks, savings banks, and private banks experienced some shrinkage, whereas loan banks continued expanding in the 20 postwar years. Particularly impressive is the increase in the number of "other banks," a category that includes the banks established or controlled from abroad.

Casting a glance at the statistics of bank offices in Table 6 the figures show, first of all, a substantial growth in the network of branches of the big banking houses. From 1947 to 1968, the number of these branch offices has grown from 182 to 428. In the case of the other groups of banks the increase in the number of offices has kept within more moderate limits.

Table 5.

	Number of banks			
	1947	1957	1967	1968
Cantonal banks	27	28	28	28
Big banking houses	5	5	5	5
Local banks	177	169	159	152
Savings banks	118	116	111	109
Other banks	56	99	167	169
Total	383	417	470	463
Loan banks	867	1,053	1,142	1,146
Total	1,250	1,470	1,612	1,609
Private banks	83	66	47	47
Branches of foreign banks	12	16	18	19
Grand total	1,345	1,552	1,677	1,675

Table 6.

	Number of banking offices			
	1947	1957	1967	1968
Cantonal banks	1,049	1,113	1,193	1,207
Big banking houses	182	217	406	428
Local banks				
Mortgage credit banks	427	511	601	558
Other local banks	344	317	273	258
Savings banks	361	364	376	376
Loan banks	869	1,055	1,144	1,148
Other banks	67	113	228	241
Deposit associations[a]	216	112	62	55
Total	3,515	3,802	4,283	4,271
Private banks	97	66	47	47
Foreign banks	12	16	18	19
Grand total	3,624	3,884	4,348	4,337

[a]Institutes of the Christian-Social Workers' Association

The economic significance of the various banking groups appears even more clearly from the balance sheet totals as listed on Table 7.

Table 7. Balance Sheet Totals

	1947		1957		1967		1968	
	Million francs	Percent	Million francs	Percent	Million francs	Percent	Million francs	Percent
Cantonal banks	9,316	39.20	15,818	37.6	36,428	30.7	39,934	28.4
Big banking houses	6,834	28.75	12,198	29.0	43,513	36.6	57,127	40.6
Local banks								
Mortgage credit banks	2,702	11.37	4,991	11.8	11,362	9.6	11,033	7.9
Other local banks	1,700	7.15	2,803	6.7	5,435	4.6	5,978	4.2
Savings banks	1,955	8.23	3,006	7.1	5,830	4.9	6,278	4.5
Loan banks	845	3.55	1,597	3.8	3,721	3.1	4,051	2.9
Other banks	416	1.75	1,671	4.0	12,439	10.5	16,143	11.5
Total	23,768		42,084		118,728		140,544	

It will be seen that the balance sheet totals of the banks covered by the statistics have increased to six times of what they had been in 1947. The growth was more than average in the case of the big banking houses, whose balance sheet totals grew more than eightfold in the 20 postwar years, and most of all in the case of the "other banks," whose balance sheet totals experienced a vigorous rise from 416 million to 16,143 million. The difference in the growth rates of the particular groups of banks resulted in a shift in the percentage distribution, which previously had shown a remarkable constancy. In earlier years it could be said that the cantonal banks and the big banking houses accounted for about one third of the grand total. By contrast in the postwar period the share of the big banking houses rose from 29 to more than 40%, whereas the share of the cantonal banks declined from 39 to 28%. The share of the smaller institutes— local banks, savings banks, and loan banks decreased from 30 to 20%, whereas the "other banks" were able to increase their proportion from 1.75 to 11.5%. As will be shown later these shifts reflect primarily the development of the foreign business, which is the special domain of the big banks and the "other banks." Accordingly the balance sheet totals exhibit a particularly swift growth since the time when convertibility was restored. The development is shown in Table 8.

From 1925 to 1935, the balance sheet totals of all banks rose at an average annual rate of 300 million francs. Between 1945 and 1950 this rate was about 1.4 billion francs. In the next quinquennium it rose to 1.8 billion, and in the

Table 8.

	Millions of francs
1906	6,350
1910	8,058
1914	9,280
1918	12,441
1920	13,840
1925	14,774
1929	20,493
1930	21,530
1932	19,945
1935	17,552
1938	18,297
1945	20,928
1950	27,385
1955	36,697
1960	56,001
1965	96,787
1966	104,834
1967	118,728
1968	140,544

Table 9.

	Gross earnings in millions of francs			
	1947	1957	1967	1968
Cantonal banks	124.33	175.3	381.0	421.8
Big banking houses	189.4	341.4	993.2	1,242.3
Local banks				
Mortgage credit banks	31.4	49.8	121.8	127.3
Other local banks	29.0	45.8	89.1	100.2
Savings banks	19.2	26.9	55.7	61.4
Loan banks	7.3	12.7	28.2	31.6
Other banks	15.0	66.7	410.5	539.6
Total	415.6	718.6	2,079.5	2,524.2
Net profits	114.0	198.1	562.9	705.2
Allotted to reserves	23.3	65.8	241.3	316.6

following years (up to 1960), to almost 4 billion. In the five years 1961-1965 the average annual growth rate of the balance sheet totals was 8 billion; in the last few years it reached 14 billion.

The earning power of the banks increased in step with the balance sheet totals. This is evident from Table 9.

Gross earnings increased from 415.6 million francs in 1947 to 2524.2 million francs in 1968. In the same time span net profits rose from 114 to 705 million. This increase was accompanied by a corresponding increase in the amounts allotted to reserves.

It is clear that this development would not have been possible had it not been for the expansion of the foreign business of the banks. Since introduction of convertibility in 1959, this line of banking business experienced a sharp upturn. From year to year the amounts deposited with the Swiss banks by foreign banks or foreign individuals increased. The banks reinvested these funds abroad because the Swiss money market was too narrow and longer-term investment of foreign money at home seemed undesirable in view of the necessity to combat inflation. Also, the banks are themselves interested in preventing a development by which their indebtedness to foreign customers would exceed their own claims against foreigners. Thus since 1960 the ties linking the Swiss banking system to foreign money markets have grown stronger and stronger (see page 103).

The coexistence of private and public institutes is typical of the Swiss banking system. Side by side with 24 cantonal banks that are organized as public banks, there are 40 local savings banks run by the municipalities. But the form of cooperative society is also widespread. No less than 1254 banks, among them primarily the rural loan associations, have elected to adopt this legal form; 294 institutes are in the form of joint-stock corporations. Taking the balance sheet total as a measure, 24.3% are public institutes, 6.3% are joint-stock corporations, and 11.7% are cooperative societies. One of the five big banking houses, the Swiss People's Bank, is organized as a cooperative society. Those in the category "other banks" are all joint-stock corporations. Among the local savings banks, we encounter all legal forms of organization.

The Swiss banking system, unlike the British system, is not specialized. Practically all institutes are universal banks—that is, banks active in all lines of banking business. This is connected, in no small degree, with the federal political structure of the country. The local and cantonal institutes endeavor to supply, as far as possible, all kinds of banking services to the populations of their regions. Hence it is not always easy to classify the individual institutes in a particular category. Of the "big five," only three can be called large-scale international trade banks. The Swiss People's Bank is a big banking house only in the sense that it has a network of branches spread over the whole country. Its balance sheet total falls short of the balance sheet total of a major cantonal bank. The inclusion of Leu and Company among the big banking houses is rooted in history rather than in anything else. That institute does not have an extensive network of branches, and should therefore be categorized rather as a major local bank. The clearest lines of demarcation, relatively speaking, can be drawn in the case of the cantonal banks. As was mentioned before, the 24 institutes in this category are full-fledged public institutes. One cantonal bank is owned by the municipalities, and in the case of three other institutes the canton is holding the majority of the stock.

The statement that all Swiss banks should be thought of as universal banks does not mean that all of them pursue all lines of banking business in the same proportions. There are considerable differences on the assets as well as the liabilities side. Thus only the three big trade banks, the "other banks," and the private banks are engaged in foreign business on a large scale. The cantonal banks, the local banks, the savings banks, and the loan banks confine themselves, by and large, to inland transactions, although we do find some foreign business even with these institutes, especially those in border regions. The big banks are primarily engaged in the financing of trade, and they are active on the international money market. This is clearly reflected in the balance sheet items Current Loans and Bills Receivable, which together amount to 34% of Total Assets. The item Due from Banks accounts for 31%; in particular, deposits with foreign banks reach a high volume. Investments in mortgages, accounting for 7%, are a comparatively insignificant item, although the two relatively medium-scale banking houses, the Swiss People's Bank and Leu and Company, do have an extensive mortgage business. By contrast, the mortgage business accounts for a large proportion—more than 50%—in the case of the cantonal banks. With these, the items Current Loans and Bills Receivable make up only 16%. Another characteristic of the business of the cantonal institutes is the item Current Advances to Public Corporations, which accounts for 8.5% of Total Assets. In the case of the savings banks and the local real estate banks, the mortgage business is naturally predominant; it amounts to more than two thirds of Total Assets. The situation is similar with the loan banks, where 61% of Total Assets represent mortgages. As for the "other local banks," one third of the assets is investment in mortgages, and another third represents trade financing. The business of the "other banks" presents a very different picture. Their extensive engagement abroad is clearly reflected in the item Due from Banks, which amounts to 37% of the total. Current Loans and Bills Receivable, amounting together to 33% have about the same relative importance as in the case of the big banking houses. Mortgage business, on the other hand, is quite insignificant with the "other banks."

Substantial differences can be found on the liabilities side as well. This is particularly true of the savings deposits, which in the case of the loan banks and the savings banks, account for 62 and 67%, respectively, of Total Liabilities, but are also much in evidence (roughly one third of Total Liabilities) with the local banks and the cantonal banks. With the big banks, by contrast, the proportion of savings deposits in Total Liabilities is only 5%, and with the "other banks" it is negligible (less than 1%). As for the big banking houses, the most important liability items are Demand Deposits (26%), Due to Banks (22%), and Time Deposits (19%). With the "other banks," the proportions are as follows: Due to Banks, 26%; Demand Deposits, 27%; Time Deposits, 22%. This points up clearly the great importance of trade financing and foreign business for these groups of banks.

Although we thus find considerable differences on the assets as well as the liabilities side, it would seem that recently the trend toward "universality" has become stronger. The cantonal banks are tending to expand trade financing, whereas in the case of the big banks, mortgage business is gaining in importance.

Mergers of banks, such as have taken place in the United States and in some European countries with the aim of creating stronger and more efficient institutes, have been rare ever since the foundation of the Union Bank of Switzerland in 1912. Some concentration in banking did come about through the years, but it was rather accidental in nature. Not infrequently minor local or private banks, for personal or financial reasons, have contacted bigger institutes and asked to be taken over by them. This explains the fact that the number of local and private banks decreased by about 70 in the 20 postwar years, whereas the branches of the big banks increased in number from 182 to 428 during the same period. One may regret the disappearance of these smaller institutes, but it

Table 10.

	Percent		Percent
Austria	4.4	Norway	4.1
Belgium	5.4	Portugal	4.0
Denmark	4.3	Sweden	5.4
France	6.3	Great Britain	3.5
Italy	6.2	West Germany	5.5
Netherlands	5.2	United States	3.4

cannot be overlooked that some regions, such as the Canton Wallis, have thereby gained access to efficient credit institutes which are better equipped to meet the needs of those regions than were the smaller local banks, whose means were naturally limited. Only in a few cases have local banks that ran into difficulties been absorbed by other local banks.

In the postwar era great demands were made on the Swiss banking system. It is pertinent to note that in the average of the years 1962 to 1967, Swiss investments reached about 27% of gross national product, as compared with 20.9% in Belgium, 21.2% in Denmark, 21.2% in France, 20.6% in Italy, 24.7% in the Netherlands, 18% in Portugal, 23.9% in Sweden, 14.8% in Great Britain, 25.2% in West Germany, and 15.1% in the United States.[11] In part this has to do with the fact that the rate of population growth was higher in Switzerland than in most other European countries. In the years 1960 to 1967, Swiss population rose 13%, from 5.3 to 6 million inhabitants, whereas other small European countries, such as Austria, Sweden, and Belgium, had growth rates of 4 to 5%, Portugal 7%, Italy 5.5%, and most of the other countries 9 to 10%.[12] The recent increase in Swiss population is partly a result of immigration. The number of foreign residents in Switzerland rose, in fact, from 285,000 in 1950 to 908,000 in 1967, without including the seasonal guest workers.

As a result the demand for housing was higher than elsewhere. As the standard of living with respect to housing is relatively high, 7.3% of the gross national product had to be allocated for these purposes in the annual average 1961 to 1966, and this does not include cost of acquisition of the lots. In 1966 the proportion was 6.8%. See Table 10 for comparisons.

[11] IMF Statistics, June, 1969.

[12] In the annual average 1958 to 1967, rates of increase in population in some countries were as follows: Austria 5.2 per mille, Belgium 6.3 per mille, Denmark 6.7 per mille, France 12.1 per mille, Italy 7.2 per mille, Netherlands, 13.3 per mille, Norway 8.0 per mille, Portugal 8.8 per mille, Spain 8.4 per mille, Sweden 6.7 per mille, Great Britain 7.1 per mille, West Germany 11.5 per mille, U.S.A. 14.5 per mille, total Europe 11.3 per mille, Switzerland 17.0 per mille. Source: UNO Annual Bulletin of Housing and Buildings, 1968.

Table 11.

	Francs		Francs
Switzerland	10,700	West Germany	2,600
Sweden	8,500	Great Britain	1,400
United States	7,500	Finland	1,200
Denmark	5,100	Austria	700
Norway	3,400	France	630
Netherlands	2,900	Belgium	600

These relationships are also clearly reflected in the mortgaged indebtedness, which per head of population is shown in Table 11.

Since 1964, the annual investments in residential building have exceeded 5 billion francs. From 1960 to 1967, about 30 billion francs were invested in residential construction without including the acquisition of lots and the cost of accessories. Only 0.5 billion francs were spent for public residential building. It is true that the Confederation and the cantons have promoted "social" residential construction by subsidies. Federal spending for this purpose amounted to 4.1 million francs in 1963, 4.9 million in 1964, 6.1 million in 1965, 20.3 million in 1966, 30.1 million in 1967, and 59 million in 1968. Credits are included in the figures for 1966 and 1967. In proportion to total annual investments of more than 5 billion francs, however, these amounts are small, even when account is taken of the fact that cantons and municipalities have allocated funds of a similar order of magnitude for the same purpose.

In most other countries the proportion of public residential building and publicly subsidized private building is higher. Thus in Sweden 44.2% and in Great Britain 50.6% of all dwelling units were built out of public funds. In Sweden about 64% of all dwelling units were built either by the government or with government subsidies. In West Germany 23% of all residential structures owe their existence to building associations or cooperative building societies, with public subsidies playing their part in nearly all cases; private residential building is partly subsidized out of public funds; part of it is not. So we see that in Switzerland investment in residential construction, although far above the international average, is nevertheless financed with a minimum of public money.

The strong influx of foreigners and seasonal workers has forced the public corporations to expand nonresidential construction in the form of roads, canalization, hospitals, and schools. As a result public construction rose from 1.7 billion francs in 1960 to 4.5 billion in 1967. For the many foreign workers, plants had to be built; this caused industrial building to rise from 1.3 to 2.4 billion francs during the period just mentioned. The great demand of industry

Table 12. Public Residential Building as a Percentage of Total Residential Construction (1967)

	Percent
Switzerland	3.6
Austria	13.7
Denmark	1.5
France	33.5
Netherlands	26.1
Portugal	12.0
Spain	8.7
Sweden (including semipublic organizations)	44.2
Great Britain	50.6
West Germany	2.9
United States	2.3

for electric power called for the construction of power-generating plants. Building costs of these plants since 1957 exceeded 400 million per year. To this must be added the cost of machinery building, estimated at 250 to 300 million francs annually. In the years 1963-64, 19 to 20% of the gross national product was spent on construction. In 1966 the percentage was still 17.6%, compared with 12.9% in Belgium, 13% in France, 11.8% in Italy, 14.2% in the Netherlands, 14.8% in Sweden, 8.9% in Great Britain, 13.4% in West Germany, and 10.1% in the United States.

Another factor straining the banking system is the huge volume of the export business which, so far as durable commodities are involved, requires medium-term or long-term financing. In 1968 Swiss exports reached 23% of gross national product. This figure is surpassed only by Belgium with 36% and by the Netherlands with 32%. Of total exports in 1968, amounting to 17.3

Table 13. Private Residential Building With Public Subsidies as a Percentage of Total Residential Construction (1967)

	Percent
Switzerland	13.0
Denmark	6.6
France	45.3
Netherlands	19.2
Sweden	32.5

Table 14. Exports of Investment Goods

Country	Total, million francs	Per head of population, francs
Switzerland	4,621	761
Belgium-Luxembourg	5,990	604
Netherlands	6,498	516
West Germany	42,780	715
United States	54,982	276
Austria	1,567	214

billion, 5.4 billion were investment goods. Comparison with conditions in other countries reveals that Switzerland has the largest export of investment goods per head of the population. The figures for 1967 are shown in Table 14.

Table 15.

	Millions of francs
Cantonal banks	2,044
Big banking houses	1,233
Local banks	
(a) Mortgage banks	532
(b) others	262
Savings banks	191
Loan banks	151
Other banks	72
Total	4,485

The financing of exports is entirely in the hands of the banks, the bulk of the burden being borne by the three big commercial banks, Swiss Credit Bank, Swiss Bank Corporation, and Union Bank of Switzerland. Thanks to the Federal export credit guarantee, the risks involved in the financing of export trade are limited.

The Swiss banking system was able to meet all demands without the Government having to intervene except for the above-mentioned subsidies to residential construction and the guarantee of credit risks on exports. It is true that the Federal Government has stated its willingness to make available to the banks the means required for the financing of residential building should such action prove necessary, but very little use has been made of this stand-by

Table 16.

	Millions of francs	
Cantonal banks	1,549	
Big banking houses	651[a]	(1579)[b]
Local banks		
(a) Mortgage banks	396[a]	(−532)[b]
(b) others	136	
Savings banks	249	
Loan banks	186	
Other banks	27	
Total	3,194	

[a]Before the absorption of three mortgage banks by a big bank.

[b]After the absorption

arrangement. The financing of residential construction by the various groups of banks is specified in the data in Table 15 which show the building credits drawn on as of the end of 1968.

Roughly one third of total current loans of the cantonal banks, mortgage banks, and savings banks is building credits. With the loan banks the proportion is more than one half, with the big banks, by contrast, it is only 21%. Looking at investments in mortgages, the importance of the cantonal banks is seen with even greater clarity. In the year 1968 mortgage credits rose as shown in Table 16.

Mortgage credits granted by the banks and outstanding at the end of 1968 amounted to 40 billion francs. Their proportion in total assets can be seen from Table 17.

Table 17. Mortgage Credits Outstanding 1968

	Million francs	Percent of total assets
Cantonal banks	20,264	50.7
Big banking houses	3,883	6.8
Local banks		
(a) Mortgage banks	7,149	64.8
(b) others	1,815	30.4
Savings banks	4,223	67.3
Loan banks	2,676	60.8
Other banks	171	1.1
Total	40,181	28.4

The way mortgages are being financed departs from what is customary in other countries. The Swiss banks finance mortgage credits partly out of savings deposits and partly by "Certificates of Indebtedness." These are securities having terms of three to five years. They are placed with the public at short intervals; this, too, is a peculiarity of the Swiss banking system. In 1968 the following sources of financing were available to the typical mortgage institutes, the cantonal banks, mortgage banks, and savings banks:

	Million francs
Savings Deposits	1,458
Certificates of Indebtedness	1,094
Total	2,552

Besides, they incurred long-term debts in the form of:

	Million francs
Bonds	354
Mortgage debentures	265
Loans from old-age and survivors insurance funds	20
Total	639

With these banks, mortgage investments and advances secured by mortgages amounted to 2614 million francs. So it is evident that sources of funds for the financing of this business sufficed. The financing of mortgage credits by savings deposits and medium-term bonds enabled the Swiss banks to make mortgages available at relatively favorable terms. Thus, interest on mortgages was 4.79% in 1968, at a time when foreign money yielded 4.04% on the average, the interest margin thus being 0.75%. The disadvantage of this way of financing is that changes in the rate of interest that occur on the money and capital market affect the mortgage credits relatively swiftly. Thus mortgage interest rose from 4.25% to 4.79% in the period 1965 to 1968. Hence the banks must reserve the right to terminate mortgage credits at short notice or to adjust them to the new level of interest rates. Another special feature of the Swiss mortgage business is the fact that a first-trust mortgage does not, as a rule, have to be amortized. Only in the case of second trusts do we frequently, though by no means always, encounter the obligation to amortize the capital. This form of mortgage financing does not conform in every respect to the classic rules of banking. The fact that it has not caused any difficulties in Switzerland can be laid to the steady rise in savings deposits, as evidenced by Table 18.

Table 18. Development of Saving With Banks (Demand Deposits, Time Deposits, Passbook Accounts)

	Million francs
1957	19,467
1958	21,174
1959	22,744
1960	24,883
1961	27,576
1962	30,345
1963	32,868
1964	35,728
1965	39,233
1966	42,211
1967	47,272
1968	53,060

The development of the commercial business is reflected in the change of the item "Current Loans" in the balance sheets of the banks. In 1968 Current Loans rose about 5 billion francs. Their distribution among the various groups of institutes is shown in Table 19.

In the 41,641 million total loans outstanding, 4485 million building credits are included. The tabulation shows the pre-eminence of the big banks in commercial business. In fact, almost one half of all current loans represented

Table 19.

	Increase in 1968	Amount in balance sheet 1968	
	Million francs	Million francs	Percent of total assets
Cantonal banks	67	9,270	23.2
Big banking houses	2,764	20,225	35.4
Local banks			
(a) Mortgage banks	107	1,967	17.8
(b) Others	60	2,394	40.0
Savings banks	53	732	11.7
Loan banks	27	407	8.4
Other banks	1,371	6,646	41.2
Total	5,059	41,641	29.5

claims by the big banks. In percentage of total assets, this item amounted to 35% in the case of the big banks, and to 40 to 41% in the case of the "other banks" and the other local banks. With cantonal, mortgage, savings, and loan banks, commercial business is of less importance.

Major items in the balance sheets of the Swiss banks are the amounts due from and to other banks. Table 20 shows the breakdown of these items at the end of 1968.

What is reflected in these figures is the high degree to which credits are interwoven, not so much within the Swiss banking system but between Swiss and foreign banks. Of the 27.4 billion francs due from banks, 19.1 billion were due from foreign banks, and of the 17.8 billion francs due to banks, 10.4 billion, certainly a large percentage, were due to foreign banks. These data show how deeply the Swiss banking system is interwoven with foreign money markets. We shall return to this point later in a different connection.

(b) The Big Banking Houses of Switzerland

The second World War has left its marks on the big banks. For years foreign business was down, and after the end of the war it was difficult to estimate the value of the foreign assets. As a result, large write-offs, which wiped out much of the latent reserves, became necessary. The Trade Bank of Basel and the Federal Bank were unable to overcome the difficulties. In proportion to the stock equity the foreign assets were so high that it would have been impossible to draw up a sound balance sheet. Therefore, as has been mentioned elsewhere, the inland business of the two banks with assets and liabilities was taken over by two other

Table 20.

	Millions of francs		
	(1)	(2)	(3)
	Due from banks	Due to banks	Excess of (1) over (2)
Cantonal banks	1,991	493	1,498
Big banking houses	17,758	12,592	5,106
Local banks			
(a) Mortgage banks	286	105	180
(b) others	534	260	274
Savings banks	143	43	100
Loan banks	724	28	696
Other banks	5,960	4,252	1,708
Total	27,396	17,773	9,623

big banks. The Swiss Bank Corporation took over the inland business of the Trade Bank of Basel. The corresponding part of the business of the Federal Bank was taken over by the Union Bank of Switzerland. Given the difficulty of obtaining a clear picture of the situation, it was by no means an easy decision for the two institutes to absorb the business of these two banks.

As we have seen only three of the remaining big banking houses can be named trade banks with international business, namely, Swiss Credit Bank, Swiss Bank Corporation, and Union Bank of Switzerland. Their French names are: Crédit Suisse, Société de Banque Suisse, and Union des Banques Suisses and this sometimes gives rise to confusion. During the postwar period the three big Swiss trade banks have greatly expanded their network of branches at home by organizing subsidiaries and taking over smaller banks. As international political conditions became more normal, these banks also reactivated their foreign business.

At the beginning of 1969, the organization of the three banks within Switzerland was as follows:

	Swiss credit Bank	Swiss bank Corporation	Union Bank of Switzerland
Establishments (including subsidiaries and head offices)	43	31	62
City branches	11	23	9
Agencies	11	33	53
Exchange offices	3	6	–
Total	68	93	124

Altogether the three institutes have 285 inland banking agencies of various descriptions. The Swiss Credit Bank and the Swiss Bank Corporation have about doubled their network of branches during the postwar period. The branches of the Union Bank of Switzerland have quadrupled.

Although a tight network of inland branches has thus come into being, the big Swiss banks have exercized some restraint in the founding of branches or affiliated institutes abroad. The Swiss Bank Corporation was the first to embark upon this venture. As early as 1898 the bank set up an office in London, then the most important financial center in the world. Even before World War I, a branch was added in West End. Since 1939 the institute has been maintaining a subsidiary in New York. A subsidiary in San Francisco followed later. The Bank Corporation controls two affiliated companies, the Swiss Corporation for

Canadian Investments Ltd. in Montreal and Toronto, and the Swiss Bank Corporation (Overseas Ltd.) in Nassau (Bahamas) with a branch in Panama. There are representatives in Paris, Madrid, Beirut, Buenos Aires, Hongkong, Johannesburg, Lima, Los Angeles, Mexico City, Rio de Janeiro, São Paulo, Sydney, and Tokyo. Since 1939, the Swiss Credit Bank has been maintaining a branch in New York and three affiliated companies: Swiss American Corporation in New York, Crédit Suisse (Canada) Ltd. in Montreal, and Crédit Suisse (Bahamas) Ltd. in Nassau (Bahamas). Representatives have been set up in London, Buenos Aires, Beirut, Mexico City, Rio de Janeiro, and Los Angeles. The Union Bank of Switzerland established a branch in London in 1967. The bank has representatives in New York, Buenos Aires, Beirut, Tokyo, Mexico City, Rio de Janeiro, São Paulo, Melbourne, Sydney, and Hongkong. The foreign establishments of the big Swiss banking houses are modest compared with those of the American banks, some of which control a network of several hundred branches all over the world. However, the big Swiss banks did not wish to compete with the foreign banks in their home territories. Thanks to their favorable location in a neutral country with a stable currency, they are being entrusted with the administration of huge amounts of foreign capital. So the foreign business has grown into substantial proportions even without the buildup of a far-flung network of branches.

In the course of the years the big banking houses have actually taken over some other banks that continued to exist as formally independent institutes. They have created financial companies of all descriptions, and have taken financial interest in mortgage banks and trust companies. Furthermore, the three big banks have a stake in international corporations that promote private enterprise in developing countries by granting advances, by participation, and by offering technical advice. On the other hand the Swiss banks, in contradistinction to some big foreign banks, do not have any controlling interests in industrial and commercial enterprises. Even their portfolio of shares of closely related financial corporations is rather limited. An exception is the acquisition by the Credit Bank in the summer of 1969 of the majority of the shares of the department store Jelmoli.

As well as the mergers that have already been mentioned, a few major financial transactions took place in the postwar period. The Union Bank of Switzerland took over the International Company for Industry and Trade (Internationale Industrie-und Handelsgesellschaft—"Interhandel") in Basel. This was a holding company, which had been founded in the interwar period by I. G. Chemie in Frankfurt, whose main asset was the General Aniline and Film Corporation in New York. Even before the war the shares of this corporation were traded on the Swiss stock exchanges. In the war and crisis years Swiss investors acquired the majority of the shares. During the war General Aniline and Film Corporation was placed under custody, as were all German and Swiss claims and interests. After the war the Swiss assets were freed but General Aniline and Film Corporation was not, for the American authorities took the position that this was a firm founded by Germans. In numerous discussions, law suits, and interventions, which dragged on through many years, the Swiss endeavored to prove that the "Interhandel" Company had been in Swiss hands ever since the end of the war and that the affiliated company should therefore be freed. However, the American authorities could not agree with this point of view. Eventually a compromise was worked out, according to which General Aniline and Film Corporation was transferred into American ownership whereas the International Company for Industry and Trade received a compensation of roughly 120 million dollars. The company used these funds for short-term and medium-term credits; in this way it became a financial corporation in its own right. In 1966 the Union Bank of Switzerland, which controlled a major portion of the stock of the "Interhandel" and whose President had worked out the compromise with the American authorities, merged with the "Interhandel" Company, whose capitalization basis was thereby broadened considerably.

The Swiss Deposit and Credit Bank in Basel and Zurich, which is controlled by the Swiss Bank Corporation, can likewise look back on a dramatic past. At the beginning of the sixties, the Spanish financier Muñoz came to Geneva. He succeeded in acquiring the majority of the Banque Genevoise de Commerce et de Crédit and later the majority of the Savings and Credit Bank in St. Gallen. The banks he controlled became involved in speculative real estate transactions which led to the collapse of both banks. Although the Geneva institute could not be saved, it proved feasible, with the cooperation of the Swiss Bank Corporation, to work out a plan under which the Bank Corporation took over the assets and liabilities of the inland business of the Savings and Credit Bank. Thanks to this arrangement, creditors of this bank suffered no losses, since at that time the original Savings and Credit Bank in St. Gallen had been in the process of liquidation. The Swiss Bank Corporation carried the inland business of the Savings and Credit Bank into a newly formed institute named "Swiss Industry Bank" (Schweizerische Gewerbebank). For technical reasons the name was later changed into Swiss Deposit and Credit Bank.

In the late summer of 1969 Swiss Bank Corporation offered to the shareholders of "Indelec" (Swiss Corporation for Electrical Industries)—a financial company in which the bank already had a controlling interest—an exchange of their shares against shares of the Bank Corporation in the proportion of 5:3. This offer, favorable as it was for the holders of Indelec shares, was accepted. Indelec in this way became an affiliated company of the Bank Corporation. The operation was accompanied by a raise in the Bank Corporation's stock equity capital, which had become necessary in view of the

Table 21.

	Swiss Credit Bank	Swiss Bank Corporation	Union Bank of Switzerland	Total 3 banks
		Millions of francs		
1950	2,265	2,670	1,699	6,634
1955	3,043	3,149	2,387	8,579
1960	4,918	5,151	4,636	14,705
1961	6,015	6,050	5,874	14,939
1962	6,806	6,878	6,961	20,645
1963	7,909	7,777	7,895	23,581
1964	8,737	8,942	8,858	26,537
1965	9,375	10,138	9,573	29,086
1966	10,223	11,294	10,122	31,639
1967	11,957	13,491	12,583	38,031
1968	15,561	16,880	18,467	50,908
Mid-1969	18,439	20,257	21,253	59,949

increase in total assets that had taken place. The stock equity could thereby be raised by 18 million, and the open reserves were augmented by about 94 million without any pressure being exercized on the capital market. Swiss Bank Corporation does not intend any merger with Indelec but is planning to maintain the company as "Banque d'Affaires" for medium- and long-term financing and acquisition of interest.

The development of the three big banking houses in the postwar era is clearly reflected in the statistics of total assets as shown in Table 21.

From 1950 to 1968, total assets rose from 6.6 to 50.9 billion francs, and the rate of growth was accelerated in the last few years. In 1968 the increase was equal to that of the 25 years between 1935 and 1960. Although up to 1961 the total assets of the five big banks (Swiss Credit Bank, Union Bank of Switzerland, Swiss Bank Corporation, Leu and Company, Swiss People's Bank) were below those of the cantonal banks, they have exceeded the latter by a substantial margin ever since, as can be seen from the diagram below. It is obvious that this vigorous growth is due to the foreign business—witness the fact that from 1960 to 1968 the connection of the Swiss banking system with foreign money markets has risen from 7 to 28.8 billion on the liabilities side, and from 7.8 to 34.4 billion francs on the assets side. Substantial funds in the form of checking accounts and deposits by banks (demand as well as time deposits) are flowing into the big banks from abroad. They are being reinvested on the Euromarket and on other international money markets. Commercial business, which accounts for about one quarter of the foreign assets, is also of importance. Furthermore the big banking houses are the receptacles for Swiss short-term

Total Assets / Liabilities of Swiss Cantonal Banks and Big Banking Houses, 1935 – 1970

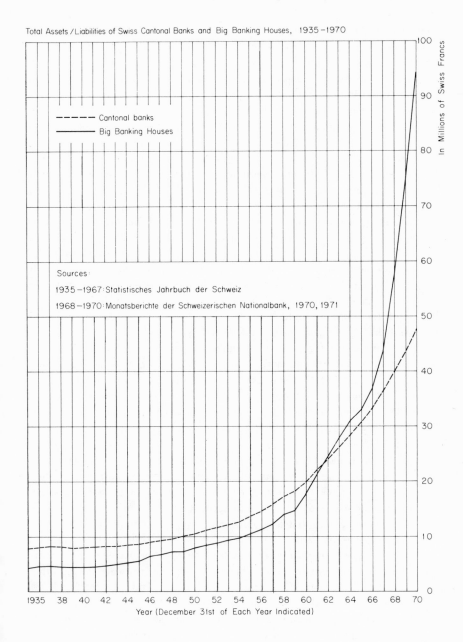

------ Cantonal banks

——— Big Banking Houses

Sources:

1935 – 1967: Statistisches Jahrbuch der Schweiz

1968 – 1970: Monatsberichte der Schweizerischen Nationalbank, 1970, 1971

In Millions of Swiss Francs

Year (December 31st of Each Year Indicated)

funds that have no adequate investment opportunity at home. These funds, too, are being invested on the Euromarket through the intermediary of the big banks. The close contacts of the banks with the foreign money markets naturally provide the opportunity for profits on interest margins. This source of income has greatly contributed to a rise in the earning power of the big banks in the last few years. Their gross earnings, which in 1960 amounted to 454 million francs, have risen to 1112 million francs in 1968. Nor is the foreign business of the big banks confined to money markets and loans. Administration of foreign funds yields earnings in the form of commission fees. Other lines of the foreign business are letters of credit, transactions in foreign exchange and in gold, syndicate operations, and activities of the banks in the capacity of trustees. As a result of the increasing connection of their business with foreign economies since 1960, the share of the foreign business in the income of the three big banks has steadily risen; and with the rise in Swiss national income, funds originating in the Swiss economy and in the Swiss banking system are likewise flowing into the big banks in ever-increasing volume. But, as already mentioned, these funds can only be invested abroad, owing to the limitations of the Swiss money market. So the relative importance of the foreign business is likely to rise further, even if the influx of foreign funds should slow down. In 1968 almost two thirds of the earnings of the big banks originated in foreign business.

In the case of the three big trade banks a comparison of the 1968 balance sheets and income statements with those of 1945 is instructive, as can be seen from the Tables 22 and 23. Total assets have risen from 4589 to 50,909 million, an elevenfold increase. The stated net profits have risen from 18.2 to 278 million. During the same period the equity capital (stock equity and reserves) was raised from 472 to 2693 million. Latent reserves may well have increased by more than 1 billion.

The three big banking houses are primarily trade banks. They grant credits to industry and to small-scale producers. Not the least important line of their activity is the financing of export trade, which in ever-increasing degree needs medium-term capital. After all, terms of settlement extending to five and even more years must be accepted nowadays. Security transactions, and the credit and stock exchange operations conducted by these institutes, likewise play a major role. As these banks are in an excellent position for placing securities, the issuing business is also important. On the whole these institutes are the ones that float new issues on behalf of foreigners in need of capital. In 1968 issues for foreign account amounted to 1089 million francs. Furthermore the big banks are being drawn into service for the granting of credits in the framework of the trade and payments agreements concluded by the Confederation with foreign countries. The banks have at times supplied huge sums for this purpose. In the autumn of 1967 the three big banking houses granted to the Bank of England a credit of 450 million francs as a contribution to the defense of the English pound. A year later this credit was assumed by the Bank for International Settlements.

The investments on the international money markets, the security transactions, and the financing of foreign trade give rise to a substantial volume of foreign exchange operations. The big banks have well-organized foreign exchange departments that are in close contact with the banks abroad. Gold transactions have gained in importance in the last few years. Trade in bank notes can look back on an old tradition (see page 96).

The big banks have always been universal banks, active in all lines of banking business. But the main emphasis is on trade financing, whereas in the case of the cantonal and local banks, mortgage financing stands in the foreground. As has been mentioned before the cantonal banks have expanded trade financing and the big banks have begun to take some interest in the mortgage business, although in the main through the intermediary of affiliated companies. In 1968 the Union Bank of Switzerland decided to take over the mortgage banks affiliated with it and henceforth to carry on the mortgage banks' business for its own (the Union Bank's) account. This was another step toward the principle of the Universal Bank. Whether this example will be followed by other institutes remains to be seen.

Although the big Swiss banks have since long outgrown the size of banking institutes of a small country, in an international comparison they occupy only (about) the fiftieth place. The total assets of the big American banks exceed those of the Swiss banks five to seven times. The large European institutes are more than double the size of the Swiss ones. The big German banks have their balance sheet totals about one and a half times those of the Swiss banks. If we look at equity capital rather than at balance-sheet totals, the comparative rank of the Swiss banks is a little higher.

In the United States, Great Britain, and France, a tendency toward concentration in the banking business could be observed during the last few years. This raises the question whether a similar development is to be expected in Switzerland. So far such a movement has never been seriously considered and is hardly to be expected in the future. A superbank, such as would come into being by the merger of two big banking houses, could hardly be accommodated in a small country such as Switzerland.

The big banks are in competition with each other, but they do cooperate in the issuing business and in the granting of current loans and advances. Thanks to the small area of Switzerland, close contacts exist between the administrations of the banks, notwithstanding the existing competition. Rates of interest and other terms are usually set after being agreed upon. The Swiss Cartel Commission, which recently investigated the situation, reached the conclusion

Table 22. Balance Sheets as of December 31, in Millions of Francs

	Swiss Credit Bank		Swiss Bank Corporation		Union Bank of Switzerland	
	1945	1968	1945	1968	1945	1968
Assets:						
Cash on hand and with the Swiss National Bank	143.1	1,574.6	105.7	1,871.7	96.6	1,847.5
Coupons	3.3	25.1	6.0	42.0	3.4	15.8
Due from banks at sight	114.5	2,376.5	123.1	3,470.8	99.6	3,130.1
Due from banks at forward dates	113.9	2,935.8	118.3	2,207.0	46.7	3,087.4
Bills receivable	294.3	1,598.7	448.9	1,492.4	143.8	1,677.4
Call loans	—	2.1	1.7	39.8	1.1	0.5
Current loans	476.6	3,915.9	393.4	3,542.9	336.3	4,448.8
Fixed loans and advances	17.9	1,679.9	40.1	2,645.2	8.4	1,380.2
Current advances and loans to public authorities	55.7	170.6	10.2	192.5	21.4	135.5
Mortgages		112.7		156.2		1,877.6
Total loans and advances to customers	550.2	5,879.1	443.7	6,536.8	366.1	7,842.1
Securities and financial interests	370.6	788.7	548.1	1,073.1	372.5	768.9
Bank premises	11.5	11.5	20.1	30.0	14.5	17.0
Other real estate	—	19.7	—	18.0	—	29.0
Other assets	4.5	349.0	10.8	98.4	12.4	51.7
Total	1,605.9	15,560.8	1,826.4	16,880.0	1,156.7	18,467.4

Liabilities:

Due to banks at sight	156.1	2,248.9	177.1	2,395.6	105.4	2,600.0
Due to banks at forward dates	—	1,496.5	—	1,623.5	—	1,943.4
Due on ground of call loans	—	0.2	—	2.7	—	—
Checking and demand deposits	795.2	3,691.1	945.6	5,309.2	599.3	4,436.4
Time deposits	128.2	3,911.9	177.8	2,723.2	86.4	3,166.6
Savings accounts, deposit books and accounts	82.8	1,332.8	106.9	1,718.4	128.7	2,582.0
Medium-term notes	189.7	1,593.3	179.7	1,534.3	109.0	1,863.4
Total deposits (excluding due to banks)	1,195.9	10,529.1	1,410.0	11,285.1	923.4	12,048.4
Bonds	—	—	—	—	—	100.0
Conversion loans	—	92.5	—	—	—	160.0
Mortgage loans	—	—	—	—	—	40.4
Checks and transit items	5.6	33.5	8.7	26.9	10.3	11.7
Drafts and acceptances	16.7	14.5	0.5	76.7	1.2	10.1
Other liabilities	36.7	360.5	33.9	613.4	23.3	474.5
Capital stock	150.0	290.0	160.0	330.0	50.0	300.0
General reserves	40.0	62.0	32.0	66.0	40.0	350.0
Special reserves	—	423.3	—	452.0	—	420.0
Carried forward	4.9	9.8	4.2	8.1	3.1	8.9
Total	1,605.9	15,560.8	1,826.4	16,880.0	1,156.7	18,467.4
Contingency obligations	43.8	476.5	45.2	546.6	79.1	727.2

Table 23. Income Statements, in Thousands of Francs

	Swiss Credit Bank		Swiss Bank Corporation		Union Bank of Switzerland	
	1945	1968	1945	1968	1945	1968
Income:						
Carryover from preceding year	4,487	6,294	4,110	7,676	2,885	6,981
Interest received	22,800	337,063	23,641	465,557	17,736	527,120
Commission fees	10,916	89,126	11,587	94,427	8,907	131,220
Income on bills of exchange	7,869	63,629	9,285	97,532	3,332	95,538
Income from securities and participations in syndicates	5,386	37,641	5,976	24,721	2,404	51,982
Income from real estate	—	1,175	—	628	—	3,501
Miscellaneous income	1,518	15,924	1,522	24,628	860	13,709
	52,976	550,852	56,121	715,169	36,124	830,051

Expenditure:						
Interest paid	10,946	247,473	10,843	344,721	8,111	391,566
Administrative expenses	24,011	163,602	27,974	224,146	18,931	257,717
Taxes and other public dues	2,376	29,716	4,107	30,041	1,485	44,109
Depreciation; Provision for reserve funds	2,186	15,000	2,570	14,216	1,946	34,741
Surplus:						
Carryover from preceding year	4,487	6,294	4,110	7,676	2,885	6,981
Net profit of the year	8,970	88,767	6,517	94,369	2,766	94,937
Total surplus	13,457	95,061	10,627	102,045	5,651	101,918
	52,976	550,852	56,121	715,169	36,124	830,051
Distribution of surplus:						
Dividends	7,500 5%	44,024 16%	6,400 4%	50,400 16%	2,500 5%	49,400 19%
Directors' fees	—	1,200	—	1,040	—	1,092
To pension funds	1,000	—	—	2,500	—	2,500
To reserve funds	—	40,000	—	40,000	—	40,000
Carried forward	4,957	9,837	4,227	8,105	3,151	8,926

that these agreements still leave enough scope for free competition and that there is thus no reason to disapprove of them.

So far as the three big trade banks are concerned, the trend of development is increasingly toward the Universal Bank, with foreign business tending to grow further. Continuation of this development is almost inevitable, even if the rate of influx of funds from outside should slow down. The more the Swiss balance of payments on current accounts tends toward closing with a surplus, the more funds flow into the big banks and must be invested by them on the Euromarket. Rising interest payments at home are matched by rising amounts of interest received from abroad. In this way the Swiss big banks are performing an important function within the framework of the Swiss as well as the international money market, but they are also incurring ever-increasing risks; and therefore they are greatly interested in the maintenance of stable political conditions in Europe, as well as in the smooth functioning of the international currency systems.

(c)   The Swiss Private Banks

In view of the expansion of the big banking houses and the foundation of numerous banks in the form of joint-stock companies during the postwar period, the question seems justified as to how the private banks, whose means are naturally limited, can still hold their own in the competitive struggle. A glance at the banking statistics shows, in fact, that in the 20 postwar years the number of private banks has declined from 83 to 47. However, this decline is partly caused by the fact that private banks have been transformed into joint-stock corporations which then carry on the existing business, frequently under the same name. Thus the private bank Dreyfus Sons and Company in Basel became a joint-stock company in 1942. In Bern the private banks Ernst and Company and Eugen von Bueren and Company took this step in 1954 and 1956, respectively. In Zurich the private banks Hoffmann, Kuenzler, Rinderknecht, Schoop, Reiff and Company, and others have been transformed into joint-stock corporations and thus are not private banks any more. Others transferred their business to big banks. Some process of selective elimination is unavoidable, especially when there are no heirs willing to continue the activities. In an anniversary pamphlet of a private banking firm we read: "Especially in the case of private banks, whose most important asset is name and goodwill, the future of the enterprise depends entirely on the presence of able successors. This fact, in conjunction with the nature of the private banking business and the unlimited liability, eventually leads to a process of selective elimination which is inevitable under competitive conditions; the process is to the advantage of the customers and, indeed, of the private banker himself."[13] In the last two decades this process

[13] Julius Baer and Company, 1890 to 1965 (Anniversary Pamphlet).

had visible effects in a reduction of the number of private banks. But banking firms that to some extent represent an old tradition and enjoy a particularly high reputation at home and abroad have survived.

In Geneva we find even today private banks that can look back on a history of more than 150 years. The banking firm of Ferrier, Lullin and Company was founded in 1798 as Ferrier-Léchet. From 1808 to 1927 its name was Ferrier L'Hoste and Company; from 1927 on it was Ferrier and fils, and still later, Ferrier, Darier and Company. The banking house Hentsch and Company was established in 1796 by Henry Hentsch; it played a significant role at the beginning of the nineteenth century.[14] Its main activity was "le commerce des étrangers." At its counters, one could see Empress Josephine, Lord Byron, and Madame de Staël. In 1800 the associate of the firm, Jean-Gédéon Lombard, with J.-J. Lullier, founded the banking firm of Lombard, Lullier and Company, which from 1826 on was named Lombard, Bonna and Company and from 1830 on was known as Lombard, Odier and Company. Under this last name the firm still exists. The fourth Geneva banking house with an old tradition is Pictet and Company. The bank was established in 1805 under the name of de Candolle, Mallet and Company. Both of these names turned up in the financial history of Geneva a century earlier. After the early death of Jacques Henry Mallet, Charles Turrettini-Necker joined the banking firm, which then continued under the name Candolle, Turrettini and Company. In 1840 Candolle took the nephew of his wife, Edouard Pictet, into the firm. The bank then carried the name of Turrettini, Pictet and Company for some time; still later it took its present name. Besides these long-established bank houses we find a number of other private banks, such as Mirabaud and Company, Barrelet, Pidoux and Company, Bordier and Company, Darier and Company, De L'Harpe and Company, Pivot and Company. Even most of these firms can look back on a history of more than 100 years. Mirabaud and Company was founded in 1819 by David Marc Paconard-Bartholomi. Bordier and Company are the successors of J. Roverdin, who was in business since 1844 as "agent de change." De L'Harpe and Company was founded in 1856 by Oumaray; Pivot and Company was established in 1869 by Grosset.

The private bankers of Geneva are organized in a "Groupement des banques privées." For the most part they are active in all lines of banking business; in the foreground stand the administration of property and the securities and credit transactions that go with it. As we have seen the Geneva private bankers have had numerous contacts with France ever since the beginning of the eighteenth century, which explains that even today they have an extensive French clientele. Thanks to its widespread domestic and foreign clientele, the "Groupement des banques privées" is in a position to place issues with remarkable ease.

[14] *Histoire de la Banque de Genève*, Geneva, 1931, p. 20.

Several times, Geneva private bankers have represented the Canton of Geneva in the Council of States. For many years the Geneva banker de Loës was President of the Association of Bankers. Representatives of the Geneva private banks, such as Alexander Lombard and Barbey, of the banking firms Lombard, Odier and Company and G. Pictet, were repeatedly in the subcommittee of the Committee on Banking at the National Bank.

In Bern, Armand von Ernst keeps up the tradition of the Bern private banks. In Basel, we encounter the name of Ehinger and Company, which turned up in Basel and Paris in earlier centuries. Likewise the private bank Labhardt and Company has a well-known name in financial history. The banking house A. Sarasin and Company, whose associate Alfred Sarasin is at this time President of the Swiss Association of Bankers, enjoys a high reputation. Other private bankers in Basel are E. Gutzwiller and Company, Heusser and Company, La Roche and Company, and Seligman-Schuerch and Company.

In Zurich, Rahm and Bodmer, and Orelli in Thalhof, can look back on a long history. In 1890, the foundation stone to the present private bank Julius Baer and Company was laid. In the course of the decades this firm, now headed by a third generation of leading personalities, has established a high reputation for itself both at home and abroad. The bank is one of the biggest private banks of Switzerland. In 1940 it founded the Baer Custodian Corporation and later the Baer Securities Corporation, both in New York. The firm is a universal bank, active in all lines of the banking business. As in all private banks, administration of property is paramount, but the bank is also active in foreign exchange transactions as well as in credit and issuing operations. Among other things the bank specializes in the trade of a variety of short-term and medium-term bonds and notes. The banking firm J. Vontobel and Company has likewise been able to attain a high standing. Today a second-generation firm, it is now under the leadership of Dr. H. Vontobel, who enjoys a high renown as President of the Supervisory Board of the stock exchange. The private bank Rued, Blass and Company, formerly Dr. E. Friedrich and Company, has proved that a private bank can create for itself a solid basis by specialization. The bank specializes in the trade of bonds and has achieved a remarkably high turnover in this business. The private bank Blankart and Company (Prop. Somary and Company) was headed for many years by Professor Somary, the well-known economist.

In St. Gallen we find the banking firm Wegelin and Company, the origin of which can be traced back to the forwarding firm that was founded by Kaspar Zilli in 1741. Transactions in bills of exchange and transactions involving loans and advances far beyond the national boundaries developed alongside the forwarding business. Ever since 1830, the main emphasis has been on banking. The political events of past decades induced the bank, which has been carrying the name Wegelin and Company since 1893, to discontinue international transactions and to devote increasing efforts to the Swiss business. Ever since that time, security transactions, underwriting, and the administration of property are at the center of the firm's activity. Since the demise of Dr. Walter Wegelin, the business is being conducted by Dr. Rehsteiner-Wegelin, who has also held the office of President of the Swiss People's Bank for some time.

Even though the number of private banks has declined in the course of the decades, it may be said that as a group they have managed to hold their own in the competitive struggle. In the future, too, the experienced private banker will have to perform his function, especially as an administrator of property or as an advisor in such administration—tasks for which the private banker is particularly well-equipped as he is in a position to consider the individual wishes of his customers.

(d) The Foreign Banks in Switzerland

Even before World War II, French banks, such as Crédit Lyonnais S.A., Banque de Paris et des Pays-Bas, and Union Bank of Alsace (Allgemeine Elsaessische Bankgesellschaft) maintained branches in Switzerland. Of the American banks, only the American Express Company in connection with its well-organized travel office was represented in Switzerland. There were also, even at that time, full-fledged banks in foreign ownership, such as the Trade Bank in Zurich. However, most of the branches of foreign banks, and banks owned by foreigners, originated in the postwar era. In the message of the Federal Council of November 1968 on the admission of foreign banks, it was stated that 102 banks with total assets of 12.5 billion francs were doubtless controlled from abroad.

Twelve foreign banks were operating 19 branches in Switzerland in the spring of 1969. The French institutes so represented are the Crédit Lyonnais S.A., Banque de Paris et des Pays-Bas, Union Bank of Alsace, Banque Ottomane, Banque de L'Indochine, Crédit Industrial d'Alsace et de Lorraine. Of the big American banks, aside from the American Express Company, the following have established branches in Switzerland during the postwar period: First National City Bank, Bank of America, Chase Manhattan Bank, and Morgan Guaranty Trust Company of New York. The main motive that induced the American banks to take this step may well have been the fact that in the postwar period many American holding companies, which wanted to use the services of American banks, were being established in Switzerland. After the First National City Bank had set up a branch in Geneva and later another one in Zurich, the other big American banks followed this example in order to avoid losing customers to the competitor.

Of the English banks, Lloyd's Bank Europe Ltd., maintains a branch in Switzerland. Other English banks have founded formally independent banking institutes. Thus the Guyerzeller Zurmont Bank is English owned; it was created

Table 24.

Year founded	Name	Stock equity Capital, millions of francs	Total assets, thousands of francs
1950	Banque pour le Commerce Suisse-Israélien	84.8	1,133,457
1919/47	Banco di Roma per la Svizzera	35.0	926,919
1952	Discount Bank (Overseas) Ltd.	36.0	840,076
1968	Banque de Paris et des Pays-Bas (Suisse) S. A.	85.0	801,073
1956	Banque pour le Développement Commercial	52.0	721,654
1965	Dow Bank AG	100.0	575,908
1957	Banca del Gottardo	20.0	445,881
1930	Handelsbank in Zurich	17.5	413,975
1959	Lavoro Bank AG	25.0	411,136
1958	Internationale Genossenschaftsbank	20.0	367,956
1922/1951	Arab Bank (Overseas) Ltd.	26.4	362,372
1938/1961	Nordfinanzbank Zurich	20.0	353,798
1961	Overseas Development Bank	20.0	272,680
1966	Wozchod Handelsbank AG	40.0	267,845
1960	United Overseas Bank	12.0	231,445
1964	Banque Scandinave en Suisse	20.0	224,339
1964	United California Bank in Basel AG	12.75	207,700
1948	Banque de Financement S. A. "Finabank"	20.0	190,505
1949	Banque pour le Commerce International	5.0	183,191
1953/1960	Cifico Bank AG	8.0	172,538
1924	Banque Privée S. A.	20.0	168,139
1960	Neue Bank	20.0	154,564
1958	Foreign Commerce Bank Inc.	10.0	139,932
1939/1959	Guyerzeller Zurmont Bank AG	5.0	113,864
1919	Banca Unione di Credito	6.0	111,806
1956	Compagnie de Gestion et de Banque, Genève	4.0	106,362
1934	Société Bancaire de Genève	10.0	104,787

in 1959 through the purchase of the New Guyerzeller Bank A.G. by the Zurmont Bank, a Montague foundation. In the summer of 1969 the British bank Keyzer Ullmann Ltd., London, set up a branch in Geneva under the name of Keyzer Ullmann A.G., with a capital of 10 million francs.

Many motives have led to founding these banks. The fact that Switzerland was able to maintain her neutrality twice during the great European wars has undoubtedly played an important part, as has the stability and free convertibility of the Swiss franc. Thus after the United States and Great Britain had blocked the Egyptian accounts during the Suez crisis, financial quarters from the Near East established banks in Switzerland in order to administer their property abroad under a neutral flag. And, as a matter of fact, the main *raison d'être* of many of the medium and small-scale banks that are controlled from abroad is to invest capital from their home country in foreign markets. These institutes have no Swiss clientele of any consequence, and they invest only a small fraction of these funds on the Swiss money and capital market. Other banks were established by foreign banks, or groups of banks, because the foreign exchange regulations at home were so restrictive they impeded the development of international business.

The liberal Swiss legislation permits the establishment of new banking institutes without any special formalities. It is true that new institutes, if they call themselves banks and take in money deposits, must submit to the supervision of the Swiss Banking Commission. But the necessity to secure a permit exists only for the opening of branches of foreign banks. In 1965 there were seven applications for such permits; two followed in 1966, and six in 1967. In 1968, when the number of applications rose to 18, the Federal Council proposed to the Legislature a tightening of the rules concerning permits for the establishment of branches of foreign banks, and it recommended the adoption of rules that would make the granting of permits a prerequisite for the foundation of formally independent banks by foreign financiers.

Some of the foreign banks developed rapidly in the postwar period. Total assets of the Banque pour le Commerce Suisse-Israélien has risen from 88 million francs in 1957 to 1133 million in 1968. In the same period, total assets of the Banco di Roma per la Swizzera rose from 247 to 927 million francs. Discount Bank (Overseas) Ltd., which was founded in Geneva in 1952, was able to increase its total assets since that time from 64 to 840 million francs. The Dow Bank A.G., founded in 1965, has a special character. The bank belongs to the Dow Chemical Complex, which maintains a large-scale holding company in Switzerland. This institute was originally endowed with a stock equity capital of 100 million francs. At first, its main line of activity was the granting of credits to the customers of Dow Chemical. The International Cooperative Bank (Internationale Genossenschaftsbank), too, is of a special nature. Founded by

European cooperative societies, the bank performs the function of redistributing and equalizing the financial resources of the cooperative banks of Europe. Then there is the Lavoro Bank, in which the Italian Banco di Lavoro is interested. Even Russia decided to set up a bank in Switzerland in 1966. In London, in Paris, and in the Near East, such institutes had long been in existence. The Wozchod Trade Bank S.A. (Wozchod Handelsbank A.G.) was endowed with an equity capital of 20 million. As early as 1968 its total assets amounted to 268 million francs. Russia's motives for founding a bank in Switzerland may have been partly political. Obviously the Soviets thought it was valuable for them to be represented in a neutral country of Western Europe that could be used as a point of departure for engaging in financial transactions and investments on European money markets. The founding of this bank was not required for the financing of the trade between Switzerland and Russia, but it is conceivable that the bank can finance the trade between Russia and other West-European countries to the extent that this cannot be performed more efficiently from Paris or London.

In the postwar period Switzerland as a financial center has been quite attractive to foreign financial quarters—much to the displeasure of the Swiss monetary authorities, who saw more drawbacks than benefits in the foundation of so many banks controlled from abroad. The increased interdependence between Switzerland and the foreign money markets, which is bound to result from this trend, could have unfavorable effects that may come to light when funds deposited from abroad are withdrawn or when they just flow back. Also, foreign banks that have agencies in Switzerland can endanger the reputation of Switzerland as a financial center by making too free a use of the freedom granted to them or by misusing the Swiss banking secret for advertising purposes. Swiss monetary and business cycle policy depends on a close cooperation between the Swiss banks and the National Bank. The greater the extent to which Swiss banking comes under the influence of foreign banks, which inevitably have less understanding of the requirements of Swiss monetary policy, the more difficult it will be to reach agreements on a voluntary basis. It was for these reasons that the Federal Council eventually deemed it necessary to tighten the control and to make the issuance of permits a prerequisite for the foundation of formally independent banks by foreigners.

(e) Foreign Exchange, Bank Notes, Gold

The convertibility of the Swiss franc, which was restricted only when and insofar as this was necessary to link imports to exports in the framework of clearing arrangements, has contributed decisively to making Switzerland a center of business transactions in foreign exchange, bank notes, and gold.

At the time of the European Payments Union, Switzerland was the only country whose currency was freely convertible in relation to the dollar. This gave the country a special position in the trade with the so-called "Provisoire Currencies," in particular, with the Transferable Account Sterling, for which Zurich was the most important trade center, ranking even before New York. As a center of foreign exchange transactions in general, Zurich shortly before the liquidation of the European Payments Union ranked third, after London and New York, with an estimated daily turnover of 250 to 300 million Swiss francs.

With the transition to convertibility, Switzerland lost her special position in foreign exchange operations. However, normal foreign exchange trade took the place of the transactions in transferable pounds and other restricted currencies. Normal transactions grew in volume along with the growing imports and exports and the growing interdependence between the Swiss money market and the money markets of other countries.

With the switch to convertibility, the members of the European Currency Agreement had to indicate to the Bank for International Settlements, which acted as agency in carrying out the Agreement, the par values of their currencies in relation to the dollar. When indicating the parities, most countries stated that they would regard as acceptable without intervention deviations from parity not exceeding ¾% on either side. This was ¼% less than the 1% maximum deviation prescribed in the International Monetary Fund agreement. Switzerland found herself in a special situation. The parity of the Swiss franc was in line with a gold price of 4920.63 francs. On the basis of a purchasing price of 4869.80 francs per kilogram of fine gold, a price of U.S.\$35 per ounce of fine gold in New York, and margins of ¼% for handling and ¾% for transportation and insurance, there resulted a lower limit of francs 4.2850 as the purchasing price of the dollar. This meant a 2% deviation from parity. As has been mentioned above, all other members of the European Currency Agreement were content with much smaller ranges of deviation. So the Swiss National Bank sought ways to narrow its range. But the Bank could not disregard the fact that the parity of the Swiss franc was anchored in gold by law, and that the rate of 4.2850 as the lower limit of the acceptable dollar price was an inevitable result, if due account was taken of the gold content of the dollar. To be sure the fact that transportation of gold by chartered airplane is somewhat cheaper than transportation by boat, which formerly was common, makes it possible to raise the lower-limit purchasing price of the dollar to 4.2950. So the margin of deviation could be set at 1¾% on either side. But this was still substantially wider than the margin admitted by any other member country of the European Currency Agreement.

In the spring of 1961, in connection with the upward revaluation of the German mark and the Dutch guilder, the problem was how to defend the Swiss franc against "bullish" speculation. At that time the management of the Swiss National Bank decided to set the purchasing price of the dollar at 4.3150, avoiding the lower rate of 4.2950 in order not to increase the unrest during the crisis. Subsequently it became apparent how difficult it was to get away from this intervention point, once it had been chosen, without again disturbing the market. So the purchasing price of 4.3150 remained in effect until the spring of 1968. It was not until the serious currency crisis which in the spring of 1968 led to a splitting of the world gold market ("two-tier system of gold") that an opportunity arose to reduce the purchasing price to the former intervention point of 4.2950. On the opposite side, the price of the dollar never rose above 4.35. Whenever the rate was 4.34 or 4.35, the Swiss National Bank sold dollars on the market, but as soon as the selling price was set above 4.35, the banks were unwilling to take dollars.

The experience is interesting in view of the widespread theory that foreign exchange rates should be allowed to fluctuate within wider latitudes. The experience of the Swiss National Bank indicates that even when the latitudes are wide, it is extremely difficult to use them in full without disturbing the market.

The Swiss National Bank allows the market a relatively wide amplitude for letting the dollar/franc rate fluctuate. The Bank did not intervene so long as the dollar stood above 4.2950 (or, between 1961 and 1968, above 4.3150). It sold dollars only when the rate exceeded 4.34 (later, 4.32). Between these buying and selling prices, the Bank leaves the dollar to the free play of supply and demand. By contrast other central banks are in the market almost daily. Thus the German Federal Bank sets the purchasing and selling price of the dollar for each day. There has been much discussion as to which system is better. In Switzerland the market has conformed to the intervention practice of the Central Bank, and the system works to the satisfaction of all concerned.

The dollar, which since the transition to convertibility has been serving as key currency generally and as intervention and transport currency in particular, plays an overriding role on the Swiss foreign exchange market. The rate of the dollar mirrors the rate of the Swiss franc. The dollar must not be thought of as fluctuating in relation to the Swiss franc; rather the Swiss franc should be thought of as fluctuating in relation to the key currency within the margins that have been discussed. In fact, since transition to convertibility, there have not been any independent exchange rates of other convertible currencies. There have only been so-called "cross rates" which can be derived on the basis of the dollar price in the country in question. Foreign exchange is not, usually, being bought and sold against Swiss francs, but against dollars, the dollar having become an international means of payment. Direct foreign exchange transactions between two European countries are rather infrequent; they come about only when supply and demand happen to offset each other. In 75 to 80% of all cases the dollar serves as the means of payment.

By contrast, forward exchange rates are being determined on the free market. Since forward sales serve in large measure to protect short-term investments abroad, they usually reflect—unless other factors are operating—

94

interest differentials such as those between investments in Swiss francs and investments in other currencies. And since interest rates for investments in francs are for the most part below those for investments in other currencies, there is, in the case of most currencies, a disagio on forward exchange. With increasing integration of the Swiss money market in the Euromarket, forward exchange transactions have greatly increased. In the summer of 1968, purchases and sales taken together exceeded 60 billion francs. So far the Swiss National Bank has not had any legal basis for operating on the forward exchange market. Since, however, such interventions may prove useful, the draft bill for a new National Bank Act provided for a closing of this gap. In 1961, when serious disturbances appeared on this market, the Federal Reserve Bank of New York, as already mentioned, was asked to buy forward dollars on the Swiss market for account of the United States Treasury.

Since the Swiss National Bank cannot take any engagements on the forward exchange markets, it is not in a position to make dollars available to the banks on a swap basis, as the German Federal Bank and the Banca d'Italia can do. The Bank was, however, able to declare its willingness to accept from the banks, at the turn of a quarter of a year, dollars on a swap basis for a few days or one month, the aim being to secure in this way the liquidity of the market over the days of the balance sheets.

Whereas the dollar as an international instrument of payment is involved in almost every foreign exchange operation, the other foreign currencies come into play only when there is a genuine demand for them, as, in particular, for payment of imports or for the financing of engagements on the money market or of other investments in the country in question. Paychecks of foreign workers have their importance, too. Switzerland's most important suppliers of commodities are West Germany, the United States, France, and Great Britain; Italy and Spain are the principal home countries of the foreign workers. Since in the raw material business the pound plays an important role even now, it ranks in foreign exchange transactions second (after the dollar), followed by the German mark, the French franc, the Italian lira, and the Spanish peseta.

Foreign exchange arbitrage has lost some of the importance it had at the time of restricted international payments. All key currencies adjust themselves in relation to the dollar, whereupon the "cross rate" can be determined immediately by a simple calculation. So there is not too much room left for arbitrage; nevertheless it is active in a fairly wide field even today.

Not all Swiss banks have the same policy in the foreign exchange business. Whereas some of them keep a set amount of dollars as reserve, others feel they can do without any open foreign exchange position. For the most part other foreign currencies are being kept only in the volume of working balances. This explains the fact that the 1967 devaluation of the pound, unlike the devaluation of 1931, did not cause any major losses.

Trade in banknotes is a business in which some banks specializing in this line were active even before the second World War. Switzerland was a "metropolis" in note trade even then; the turnover was greatest in French francs, in lire, and in pesetas. Today the total turnover in notes is estimated at 1.5 to 2 billion francs per year, which means that Switzerland may well have to be regarded as the world's biggest center of trade in banknotes. This is partly due to the fact that Switzerland has no regulations regarding import and export of notes. The low rates of interest make it possible for the banks to hold relatively large stocks of notes. The central location of the country, the good airline connections, and the world-wide contacts of the banks with foreign countries have favored this development. In the postwar era the extensive tourism and the foreign workers have given additional impetus to the trade in notes, and the periodic currency crises have also contributed. At the beginning of the travel season, demand for European and North American bank notes rises, the currencies most sought being the lira, the peseta, and the French franc. At the end of the season, part of the notes flows back. At the close of the year, demand by foreign workers for bank notes in the currencies of their home countries makes itself felt quite distinctly.

Although, in general, the exchange rates of bank notes fluctuate within narrow limits only—paralleling, as a rule, the rates of the bills of exchange—the fluctuations may assume substantial proportions in times of currency crisis and foreign exchange control introduced in connection with it. Thus in the crisis of mid-June 1968, the French notes exhibited a disagio of almost 1% in relation to parity. Hence, trade in bank notes is not without risk, all the more so as counterfeit notes creep into circulation from time to time.

Trade in gold is a line of business in which the Swiss banks have always been active, although in prewar times this line did not have the importance it has today. After the second World War, Switzerland developed into a full-fledged gold trade center. This is due to the fact that the banks took up the gold business immediately after the war in 1946, whereas the London gold market was reopened only in 1954. Gold trade, which is frequently conducted on a credit basis, has been helped by the relatively low rates of interest in Switzerland and by the abolition of the sales tax. The large and steadily growing foreign clientele of the Swiss banks has likewise given the gold trade some impetus. Further favorable factors were the central location of Switzerland and the absence of restrictive foreign exchange regulations.

When the London gold market was reopened in 1954, Zurich was already established as a center of gold trade. Due to the fact that London, acting as agent for South Africa, brought South Africa's gold to the world market, the British capital was able to recapture a central position in gold trade. But since it is forbidden to own gold in England, the metal traveled from London to the international markets, the Swiss big banks acting as intermediaries. As a rule they handled about three quarters of the gold supply. Through the big Swiss banks, the gold bought in London went to foreign markets. The Swiss customers of the banks were not interested in holding gold, at any rate not before the great gold buying wave of winter 1967-68. They preferred to invest their savings in interest-bearing securities. Even today, the most important marketing areas for gold are the countries of the Middle and Far East, where gold has for centuries been the medium for investing capital. About one quarter of the gold purchased by the Swiss banks goes into these regions. As a rule, 10 to 15% is taken by French customers; about 10% goes back to English gold brokers, and 5% goes to German investors. A fraction is absorbed by the Swiss watch and jewel industries, and the rest goes to gold dealers at home, who in their turn export the metal. Since, as has already been mentioned, each of the three big Swiss banks that are engaged in the international gold business controls a gold refinery, they were able, during the wave of heavy demand for gold, to offer gold not only in normal bullions, but in kilogram bullions as well as in smaller units. But since then the demand has fallen off considerably.

Zurich has even increased in importance as a center of gold trade because of the split of the gold market in the spring of 1968 and the decision of South Africa to sell no more gold on the London market as a matter of routine. Since that time the supply of gold no longer comes, in the main, from new production, but rather from sales by private individuals who acquired gold during the gold buying wave of 1967-68. Thanks to the large foreign clientele of the big banks and the substantial supply of gold the banks are holding, it is safe to say that Zurich has become the most important gold market in existence. Today the gold business is handled, in considerable part, on a bookkeeping basis. The banks buy and sell gold without any gold bullion being shipped. This way of performing the transactions presupposes a large clientele in which both buyers and sellers are active, and an adequate supply of gold in the hands of the banks. At present, both of these prerequisites are actual facts in the case of the Swiss banks. And so a gold price emerges in Zurich even before the fixing in London; this Zurich price serves as a guideline to the English brokers and is usually accepted at the London fixing. Some Swiss banks have specialized in the gold coin business. They are in a position to satisfy demand for all gold coins and gold medals in current use.

(f) Banking Legislation and the Swiss Bank Secret

Until the middle of the nineteen thirties, Switzerland had no legal regulation of banking on the Federal level. The cantons did issue such regulations, partly in connection with the establishment of cantonal banks. Protection of savings deposits was the primary purpose. Federal legislation confined itself to bank notes and later to the Federal Act on the Establishment of the Swiss National

Bank. In September, 1914, and in June, 1932, a Federal Resolution about the creation of a Federal Loan Bank was made public. In June 1930 a Federal Act on the issue of mortgage debentures was passed. The Federal Loan Bank was conceived of as an agency supporting banks in distress. In the war and crisis years it repeatedly granted credits to banks in difficulties, thus enabling them to survive in the critical years. In the postwar period the Loan Bank could be liquidated.

The crisis years after 1931 accelerated the pace of legislation in this field, especially after the Federal Government had found it necessary to support two banks. The Federal Act of 1934 on Banks and Savings Banks reflected liberal principles. Its main purpose was the protection of creditors of banks. The constitutional basis for the Bank was Article 34 and (since 1947) the new Article 31(4), of the Federal Constitution. Of the provisions purporting to protect the creditors, the following stand out: rules on the internal organization of banks; on liquidity; on internal sources; on the setup and publication of annual financial statements; on the priority rights of savings deposits; on receivership proceedings; on auditing; on the distribution of responsibilities. The Federal Banking Commission was created as the supervising agency. The auditing takes the form that all institutes under the Bank Act must each year allow a trust company of their choosing to look into their status. It is incumbent on the trust company to see that the rules of the Bank Act are observed. In case of violation, the trust company takes the necessary measures; only upon repeated non-compliance with the law is the trust company obligated to notify the Banking Commission, which then intervenes. This supervision sufficed so long as the managements of the banks, mindful of the interests of their clientele, made it a point to keep strictly within the law. But it failed in the case, already mentioned, of the Savings and Credit Bank of St. Gallen when the holder of the majority of the shares tried to use the bank for his own personal advantage. The new bill on banking which is now under consideration has drawn certain inferences from this experience.

In Articles 7-10 the Bank Act has provisions with objectives that lie in the field of credit and monetary policy. Thus under Article 8, authorization by the National Bank is required for capital export in the form of public issues or bank credits, if the latter exceed 10 million and their terms exceed two years. The National Bank examines an application for permit from the viewpoint of the money and capital market, and submits it to the three interested Federal departments in order to be able to take account of objections or conditions suggested by general economic policy. Since its revival after the second World War, capital export was only disallowed in 1956 for a time, because of a strained condition that existed then in the capital market. Since the National Bank keeps the banks informed on the extent to which it is willing to authorize capital exports, the institutes concerned can set up plans in the framework of which the permit procedure usually functions smoothly. Under Article 10, the National Bank must be informed about any contemplated raise of the interest rate on demand deposits. The Central Bank has no veto power supported by sanctions; after the end of a waiting period, a bank may raise the rate of interest despite an objection by the National Bank. This, however, occurs only rarely. In general, an objection raised by the Central Bank is heeded, all the more so as the policy of the Bank merely aims at moderating the pace of change and preventing individual bank managements from acting rashly.

Another set of provisions has for its goal the protection of the bank itself and, thereby, the protection of its stockholders. Thus in case of difficulties in keeping up payments at maturity, the banks are granted a respite or, in analogy to bankruptcy procedure, a moratorium. Actions willfully damaging credit are punishable under a separate provision.

The foundation of banks is not subject to any permit procedure. But whoever wishes to start a banking business and to take in deposits must first contact the Banking Commission which then decides whether the new institute is to come under the Banking Act or not. The Commission has to inquire whether the new institute has an organization that makes the smooth handling of banking transactions possible. Only if the Banking Commission confirms that this is the case can a new banking firm be entered in the Trade Register. Affiliates of foreign banks do, however, require a permit because the case of a branch is a special situation, as the parent institute is able to influence the business policy of the affiliate. In the permit procedure, the supervising authority may set certain conditions for the granting of the permit.

The draft for a revision of the Bank Act provides that the revised Act will cover, in addition to banks, banklike financial companies. In a way the draft makes the foundation of new banks more difficult. With respect to foreign-controlled banks, it incorporates, pursuant to a Federal Resolution of March 21, 1969, the special provisions of the existing Bank Act, but with the additional rule that a bank which comes under foreign control after its foundation must secure a supplementary permit. The supervising agencies have to be watchful in regard of the prerequisites of permits and have to notify the Banking Commission more promptly than under the present Act of any irregularities.

With a view to protecting the customers of the banks, Article 47 sets down rules regarding the bank secret. Again and again, this gives rise to regrettable misunderstandings. After all, it is regarded as a matter of course all over the world that banks should keep their business relationships with their customers confidential. Like the physician and the lawyer, the banker could not possibly fulfill the tasks of his profession if he did not in this respect behave as he is generally expected to. The Swiss bank secret differs from that of other countries only in that its violation is a punishable offence. But Austrian and French laws have similar penal clauses. Nor is the Swiss bank secret absolute. It affords no protection in cases of offenses covered by the penal code or by receivership and bankruptcy laws.

The so-called "numbered accounts," which are often believed to be anonymous accounts, have likewise contributed to the rise of legends. Actually no bank can open an account without knowing who the customer is. With a view to the case of death, if for no other reason, the bank must know who stands behind a numbered account. The only purpose of these accounts is to reduce the number of bank employees who know the depositor's identity. The numbered accounts appeared first in the nineteen thirties, when in some countries it was forbidden under the most severe penalties to hold assets abroad, but at the same time many persons had to be prepared to leave their homeland for political or racial reasons. To many of these persons a small amount of savings deposited on the other side of the frontier could under certain circumstances be a life or death matter. At that time a host of agents whose assigned job it was to track down such assets swarmed all over Switzerland. And, in fact, as is clearly evident from the records of the debates, Article 47 of the Bank Act of 1934 is directed primarily against espionage in banking.

A sovereign nation cannot permit officials of another country to exercise supervisory functions on its own territory. When, for example, American banks have set up branches in Switzerland, the latter are under Swiss law, just as branches of Swiss banks established in the United States are under American law. So the American supervising agent, who looks into the business of banks operating there, has no right to supervise the branches of these banks operating in Switzerland. This rule is in agreement with the territorial principle that is anchored in international law. The American authorities, too, had to recognize this rule in the lengthy negotiations that took place. Thus Switzerland cannot tolerate foreign supervising agents on her territory, nor can she apply foreign law, or discriminate against foreign citizens. But she is willing, within the framework of her own legal system, to cooperate with other countries in law enforcement, as, for example, when provisions of the Swiss Penal Code have been violated.

Concerning the questions that interest the fiscal authorities, we have to do, not with a special property of the Swiss bank secret, but rather with a property of the tax law which rests on the principle of self-declaration. The government does not claim any right to look into bank accounts. This agrees with the Swiss view according to which a citizen has a right to a clearly defined area of privacy which must be respected by the Government. "In the view of our people," declared Mr. Bonvin, member of the Federal Council, at a press conference held in 1967 before representatives of foreign newspapers, "the freedom of the

100

individual takes precedence over the fiscal interest, even on the risk that this freedom is sometimes misused." It would seem that in a world in which the role of the government and its fiscal authorities becomes ever more dominant, there is not too much understanding for such protection of an area of individual freedom. Switzerland does not wish to allure any foreign tax evaders with her bank secret. Money that has such an origin is neither needed nor welcome in the country. However, being a nation based on law, Switzerland cannot treat the foreigner differently from the way she treats her own citizens. In the field of taxation, there is thus not much room for judicial assistance to other countries in enforcing their law.

But since the Swiss authorities and banks do not like to see foreign citizens violating the law of their own country under the shelter of Swiss legislation, they are generally willing to cooperate in the search for a solution, provided that no principles of Swiss law are thereby disregarded. Thus the big Swiss banks have always drawn the attention of American citizens to the fact that the purchase of gold is against American law; some banks even went to the length of declining such orders. Sometime ago, a conflict with the United States threatened to arise because a bank established in Zurich but controlled from abroad had violated American regulations concerning loans on American securities. Under Swiss law the bank was under no obligation to obey these regulations. The Swiss Government could not intervene as it had no legal basis for doing so. But the Association of Swiss Bankers sent a circular to the Swiss banks recommending that they take into account, as far as possible, American regulations with respect to loans on securities. Thus in individual cases it is always possible to find acceptable solutions even paying due respect to national sovereignty and existing law.

2. The Money Market and the Capital Market

(a) The Money Market

In the postwar period the Swiss money market had a relatively high degree of liquidity. With the big banks, cash on hand, credit balances on drawing accounts, and balances on postal cheque accounts amounted in September, 1958, to 1.8 billion francs, or 13.6% of total assets. In the following years, liquid assets did not keep pace with the rise of other assets. In September, 1968, they were 4.7 billion, or roughly 9% of total assets. This development must be viewed in the context of the radical changes that took place on the European money market—as, indeed, all problems of the Swiss money market can only be understood in this wider framework. In times of strained political conditions, or disturbances in the international currency situation, funds from abroad would flow into the Swiss banks again and again. The incoming dollars would then be transferred to the National Bank, which had to supply Swiss francs in return. In this way the market became extremely liquid, which made it necessary for the National Bank to siphon off some of the liquidity. Thus in 1960 "sterilization bonds" amounting to 400 million francs, were placed on the market, and in the spring of 1961, 1 billion francs held by the banks as balances on drawing accounts were blocked in a special account with the National Bank. Under the impression of these events, the Swiss observer in the "Club of Ten" suggested as late as 1963 the creation of an international money market as an instrument for channeling the inflowing funds back to where they came from. At that time we believed, in fact, that it was necessary to create such a money market by special international action. In the meantime, however, an exchange of funds within the European banking system developed without the monetary authorities taking any action, and the importance of this exchange increased from year to year. In 1963 Italy ran into difficulties with her balance of payments, but the difficulties became manifest only months later; for in the meantime the Italian banks had obtained credits from banks of other countries and this had made it possible to finance the deficit without having to draw on the currency reserves.

These events induced the European central banks, as participants in what came to be called "Multilateral Surveillance," to notify the Bank for International Settlements not only of changes in currency reserves, but also of changes in the external positions of the banks. These figures were exceedingly instructive. They showed that changes in the positions of the banks increased in importance from year to year, whereas the significance of changes in the currency reserves declined more and more. What we were witnessing here was the rise of the so-called "Euro-Money Market." This is an international money market in which the banks of countries having balance of payment surpluses play thy role of money suppliers, and the banks of the deficit countries play the role of money absorbers. This market thus contributes greatly to an international leveling of liquidity. The volume of the market was estimated at more than 30 billion dollars in 1968. Value judgments on the market have varied greatly right from its beginning. It has been pointed out that those who ultimately receive short-term funds are apt to tie them up in long-term investments, and that the market is a channel through which money supplied by the central bank flows back into the economies of the countries in question. On the positive side we have the fact that for the countries participating in the market, surpluses and deficits in their economic position vis-à-vis other countries are being evened out through the intermediary of the market. As a result the reserves of the central banks can recede into a second line of defense. The fact that, contrary to the expectations of many monetary experts, international liquidity has so far remained adequate, may well be due, in part, to this market.

Table 25. Claims and Debts of the Swiss Banks vis-à-vis Foreign Countries

	Claims	Debts
	Millions of francs	
Year end, 1960	7,800	7,000
Year end, 1965	18,300	16,900
Summer, 1968	31,870	27,700
Year end, 1968	34,400	28,800
Summer, 1969	40,200	34,500

On the other hand the liquidity reservoir which the market represents may have unfavorable effects on the currency system, as has proved to be the case in the gold and the German mark speculation of 1968 and 1969. Thus light and shadow are lying close together. In any case the market can no longer be imagined away as it does satisfy an actual need.

In due course the Swiss banks ceased to sell inflowing foreign exchange to the National Bank; instead, they invested these funds on the Euromarket. The National Bank had to deal less and less with hectic inflows such as had been seen as late as 1960 and 1961. At the same time the Swiss banking system became more and more interwoven with the international market. The development stands out clearly from the figures shown in Table 25.

Except for very extraordinary circumstances, dollars are at present being offered to the Swiss National Bank only when the banking system lacks a desirable degree of liquidity, as may well be the case on the date of the balance sheet. Hence the currency reserves of the Bank rise less sharply now than they did in former years. Whereas in the period 1956-1962, they increased from 7.4 to 11.4 billion—that is, more than 50%—in the following six years the rate of

Table 26. Currency Reserves and Foreign Accounts of the Swiss National Bank (Millions of Francs)

	Gold and foreign exchange	Deposits, not subject to exchange rate fluc- tuations with foreign central banks	Foreign treasury bonds	Total
Sept., 1966	12,600	519	432	13,611
Sept., 1967	13,634	174	432	12,240
Sept., 1968	12,659	360	1,442	14,461

increase slowed down to 15%. We must remember, though, that other forms of currency reserves—American Treasury bonds in Swiss francs, deposits hedged against exchange rate fluctuations with foreign central banks—have increased by roughly 1.5 billion francs since 1962. Tables 26 and 27 tell how the currency reserves of the central Bank and the positions of the banks have developed from autumn, 1966 to autumn, 1968.

Here the contrast between the dynamics of the positions of the banks and the relative stability of the reserves of the central Bank is quite striking. Changes in the currency reserves and in the position of the banks vis-à-vis foreign countries reflect, to a certain extent, the "net" of a country's balance sheet in relation to the rest of the world. In the case of Switzerland the picture may be somewhat distorted by financial operations of foreign holding companies, of insurance companies, and of big Swiss industrial concerns. Yet the inference seems legitimate that in the period from autumn 1966 to autumn 1968 the country's balance sheet relative to the rest of the world must have closed with a huge surplus. The involvement with foreign economies is, in fact, somewhat greater than it appears from these figures, as the banks have maintained credit balances with the Bank for International Settlements and have taken single bills of exchange from this institute. In the autumn of 1968 these balances and bills of exchange added up to 1.1 billion francs. The pace of this development has accelerated in the last few years. Whereas from 1960 to 1965 the foreign claims and debts of the Bank grew to the tune of 1.8 to 2 billion annually, the two following years showed annual rates of increase of more than 4 billion; in 1968, the increase was even 9 billion. At the same time the excess of these assets over these liabilities rose from 952 million francs in 1966 to 5038 million in 1968. Had it not been for the international money market, the Swiss currency reserves would probably be markedly higher today.

At the end of each year the banks, striving for an adequate degree of liquidity, find themselves motivated to transfer dollars to the National Bank. As has already been mentioned the Bank is willing at any time to take dollars from the banks on a spot basis as well as, for a brief period, on a swap basis. As a rule

Table 27. Claims and Debts of the Swiss Bank vis-à-vis Foreign Countries (Millions of Francs)

	Claims	Debts	Balances
Sept., 1966	17,662	16,710	952
Sept., 1967	23,241	21,115	2,126
Sept., 1968	32,500	27,462	5,038

the dollars temporarily deposited in this way with the Swiss National Bank are being invested by the Bank on the Euromarket, either directly or via the Bank for International Settlements. The purpose is to cushion the disturbances caused by the year-end operations of the Swiss banks. In the last few years the volume of these dollar swaps over year ends attained about 1.5 billion francs. In 1968 it rose to more than 3 billion.

The ever-increasing involvement of the banks in the foreign money markets, the rising order of magnitude of the entries in the balance sheets of the banks, and the resulting great need for liquidity at balance sheet dates have recently brought about the necessity of liquidating foreign investments not only at year end, but even at the ends of quarters. Thus the National Bank at the end of March, 1969, had to take dollars equivalent to nearly 1 billion francs and to open credits on securities or on bills of exchange for about the same amount. In this way the close ties between the Swiss money market and the international markets result in a steady influx and outflow of funds with corresponding fluctuations in currency reserves. The higher the interest rates on the Euromarket, the more the banks are inclined to invest their liquid funds on this market. This may lead to a noticeable tightening on the Swiss money market each time before the close of a quarter. Thus at the end of March, 1969, the rate of interest on the Euromarket went up to 9% for Swiss francs (daily allowances; in swap transactions the rate was considerably higher). After the close of the quarter, the rate fell back to 3½%. This is the "reverse side" of a small money market being very tightly interwoven with the markets abroad.

Measured by comparison with the levels of the claims and debts of the banking system in relation to foreign markets, the figures relating to the domestic money market appear rather small. Short-term treasury bills, a type of security most characteristic of large money markets, are missing on the Swiss market. The Government does not issue securities having terms of three months. The shortest maturity term for Government bonds is one year; there are also issues having terms of one-and-a-half to two years. Among the Government bonds there are, to be sure, some 80 million francs which the banks can deposit with the National Bank at any time for a shorter or longer period. These bonds are therefore suitable for investing cash on hand. But this has been made possible only thanks to the intervention of the National Bank. At the end of 1968 Government bonds in the market amounted to 889 million francs. Also, the cantons issued bonds amounting to 70 to 80 million. In order to compensate, at least to some extent, for the lack of three-months bills, the Federal Government issues its bonds two weeks after the close of each quarter. This enables the banks, by appropriately "staggering" their bond holdings with an eye to maturity dates, to have maturing bonds at each quarter. As the total volume of the bonds on the market is small, they change hands very rarely. For the most part these bonds are in the portfolios of the big banking houses where they serve as a welcome addition to liquid assets.

Motivated by the massive influx of money in 1960, the National Bank, as has already been mentioned, placed on the market so-called "sterilization bonds" of the Federal Government in the amount of 400 million francs. The amount issued rose later to 600 million but declined to 375 million in 1968. Formally, these are Government securities; actually, however, they represent a liability of the central Bank, which issues them and is responsible for the interest payments on them. At the close of each year, and in part also at balance sheet dates, they can be deposited with the National Bank for a few days. By issuing money market securities of this kind, the Swiss National Bank pursues two different aims. One purpose is to siphon off excess liquidity from the money market. The second is to induce the banks to secure the liquidity required on balance sheet dates by transferring such bonds rather than by operations on the foreign exchange market. Most of the money market securities of the National Bank have terms of one to two years. A minor fraction is redeemable after three months.

At the end of 1968, the Banks' total holdings of what might be categorized as money market instruments was 6,859 million francs. Of these 1508 million were foreign bills of exchange. Of the domestic papers 1085 million francs represented Federal and cantonal bonds (including the money market bonds issued by the National Bank). This leaves us with only 4266 million domestic bills of exchange. Of these 1036 million had been created as instruments of a war economy to finance inventories; they are being renewed each time they fall due. So the commercial bills receivable amounted to 3230 million francs only and even of these, 1520 million were single bills of exchange issued by the Bank for International Settlements. These latter are counted as inland paper; economically, however, they represent investments abroad since the counter-vailing amounts were invested in other countries by the Bank for International Settlements. In relation to total assets of the banks—more than 140 billion francs—the total holding of inland bills receivable and money market bonds is thus quite small.

Normally the banks use the credit facilities available through the National Bank only in small measure and, for the most part, only temporarily at dates of the balance sheet. Thus apart from these dates, the Bank's portfolio of bills of exchange in the year 1968 was mostly under 100 million francs, of which nearly 80 million were "inventory bills" of the type described above. Commercial bills in the proper sense thus kept at a level of, predominantly, less than 20 million francs. Credit on securities was used to the tune of 27 million francs in the average of the year. It is only at the close of a quarter or a month that the credit of the central Bank is being drawn upon in larger measure. At the end of October, 1968, the portfolio of bills of exchange rose to more than 300 million francs; at the end of December it again reached the level of almost 290 million, and at the end of June, 1969, it grew to 1137 million. At the last-named date, the total volume of central Bank credit used was 1443 million francs.

Since the Swiss money market lies, in large part, outside the frontiers of the country, the Swiss banking system is very much dependent on a stable exchange rate of the franc. A flexible exchange rate of the type proposed at present in scientific quarters would be bound to result in considerable difficulty in investing liquid funds on the international money market, and would expose Swiss economic relations with the rest of the world to the chance fluctuations of money market operations. A small nation with so manifold ties linking her economy to other economies cannot afford to experiment with flexible exchange rates.

(b) The Capital Market

As a rule, the Swiss capital market can meet the needs of the domestic economy and, moreover, make capital available to foreign economies. This is reflected, first of all, in the rates of interest which, for the most part, are below those prevailing abroad. Thus at the end of 1968 the yield of Federal bonds was 4.33%. The yield of cantonal bonds was 4.66%. The yields of comparable government bonds in some foreign countries were as shown below:

Country	Percent
Belgium	6.63
Denmark	8.83
Germany	6.30
France	7.41
Great Britain	7.99
Italy	5.62
Sweden	5.88
United States	5.65
Canada	7.45

There was thus a difference of 1.3% in relation to the United States, and one of about 4% in relation to Denmark. At the beginning of 1969, new loans could be floated at 5% on behalf of cantons and cantonal banks, and at 5½% on behalf of power plants and industries, as well as for foreign firms in need of capital. The Federal Government could go to the market offering 4¾%.

This was not always so. In 1848 when the Confederation wanted to issue her first loan in the amount of 3.3 million francs, she knocked in vain at the doors of Paris and Frankfurt. From that time dates an anecdote. In the course of a talk on the possible granting of a loan, Mr. Rothschild, banker in Frankfurt on the Main, is said to have asked a Swiss delegate how the bonds of the Confederation were quoted on the stock exchange. The man from Switzerland could not answer the question as the Confederation at the time did not as yet have a public debt. The story goes on to tell that this did not by any means satisfy Rothschild. The absence of any government securities seemed to him to indicate bad credit rating. The loan was eventually floated at home, but it took several months before the amount was fully subscribed.

No matter how reasonable the interest rates now prevailing on the Swiss capital market may appear in an international comparison, they are nevertheless high when compared with rates in former years. In the period 1949 to 1955, the Federal Government could reach the market with 3%; in 1954, even with 2¾% on two occasions. It was not until 1966 that the government had to offer 4½%; in 1967, 5% had to be offered. The low interest level of the postwar era is partly explained by the fact that investment demand and the consumption of electrical energy in the economy were still relatively low. There was as yet no need for new power plants. In 1948, moreover, old age and survivors insurance, whose equalization fund had more than 500 million francs available for investment each year, went into effect. At times it was so difficult to find investment opportunities for this money that the fund had to ask the Federal Government to take some. Now since the government had no deficit on current account, it could use those funds only for debt repayment. The dearth of investment opportunities for the money available to the old age and survivors insurance fund was such that there was a serious question as to whether the fund was about to become the principal creditor of the government; at the same time this would rid it of indebtedness on the public market. But a few years later the picture changed totally. The old age and survivors insurance fund became a much-sought source of investment capital; it was being tapped by municipalities, cantons, banks, and power plants. In 1956 the situation on the capital market was so tight that the National Bank had to restrict capital exports for a while. The overheating of the economy in the years 1962 to 1965 drove the interest rates upward. Taking the yield of the Federal bonds as a measure, the peak was reached at the beginning of 1967 with a yield of 4.74%. In the course of the two following years the yield could be reduced to 4.33%, but it rose again to 5.37% in September, 1969.

The relatively low level of interest rates is all the more surprising as the rate of investment is higher in Switzerland than in most other countries. In fact, 27% of the gross national product is being used for investment purposes. If we wish to investigate the causes of the efficiency of the Swiss capital market, we must try to get a picture of the components that make up supply and demand.

In the year 1966, which was still under the aftereffects of the economic overheating of the preceding years, 17.5 billion francs were required for investment in nonresidential capital goods (exclusive of cost of sites) of which 11.3 billion were for new structures, 5.8 billion were for machinery and equipment, and 0.4 billion were additions to inventories. Private residential building required 4.3 billion francs, to which must be added 1.2 billion for purchase of lots and for development costs. The total investment of 5.5 billion was financed as follows:

	Billions of francs
Mortgage credits granted by banks, total amount slightly above 2.7 billion, of which for residential construction	2.20
Advances by banks, covered by mortgages	0.25
Contributed by life insurance companies and pension funds	0.60
Contributed by public authorities (estimate)	0.05
Total financing from external sources	3.10

Internal financing thus amounted to 2.4 billion francs. Of these, 400 million were raised by the insurance companies to finance construction of their own buildings, which means that roughly 2 billion had to be raised by private individuals.

The amount invested in the same year for industrial purposes was 7.8 billion francs, of which 2.4 billion were for industrial establishments, 0.45 billion for power plants, 4.5 billion for machinery and equipment, and 0.45 billion for additions to inventories. The sources of the invested funds were the following:

	Billions of francs
Bonds issued on the market	
by private business	0.118
by power plants	0.554
New stock capital	0.900
Mortgaged credits	0.660
Total financing from external sources	2.232

We thus see that 5.6 billion had to be raised by business from internal sources. Undistributed profits contributed 2.5 billion, depreciation allowances 3.3 billion, which adds up to 5.8 billion.

In the public sector, 5.1 billion were invested, of which 3.85 billion were spent on structures and 1.25 billion on machinery and equipment. Most of the money spent on machinery and equipment was spent by the Swiss Federal Railroads, by the Post, Telegraph, and Telephone Administration, by the communication agencies, and by the public enterprises of the municipalities.

To finance these investments, bonds amounting to 1152 million francs were issued by public authorities. The banks granted credits totaling 345 million francs. Old age and survivors insurance and other public funds have probably contributed 250 million, and the insurance companies and pension funds, 100 million. Total external financing thus amounted to 1847 million francs, which means that 3.3 billion had to be raised by the public agencies themselves. The Federal Railroads and the Post, Telegraph, and Telephone Administration raised about 1 billion. The Federal Government made about 1 billion francs available for its own buildings and for road construction by the cantons. The cantons themselves and the municipalities raised 1.3 billion francs.

For miscellaneous construction not falling under any of the categories discussed so far 0.4 billion was required. This was spent on, among other things, investments in private railways, private roads and canalizations, sporting establishments, and so on. Here the sources of financing cannot be broken down in detail. In part, subsidies by public authorities were available.

We see that of the aggregate investment of 18.7 billion francs (including 1.2 billion for acquisition of lots), 7.1 billion were financed from external sources, and 11.6 billion francs, from internal ones.

The capital market was drawn upon in the following proportions:

	Billions of francs
Bonds issued on the open market (net)	2.318
Loans not issued on the open market	0.446
New share capital issued	1.279
Total amount contributed by saving via security purchases	4.043

Of the total, 0.560 billion represented loans for foreign account. The balance, 3.483 billion or, rounded, 3.5 billion, was available for Swiss requirements.

Summing up, the following sources were available for external financing:

	Billions of francs
Saving through deposits of various descriptions with banks, totalling 2.9 billion; deducting 0.6 billion used for purposes other than investment, there remained	2.3
Repayment of mortgages	1.3
Saving through purchase of securities	3.5
Saving through insurance outside the market for securities	0.5
Total	7.6

The fact that investment was relatively high without any undue pressure on the capital market is explained by the high power of internal financing displayed by both the private and the public sector.[15] In the private sector, internal financing as a percentage of total financing is probably higher in Switzerland than in most other European countries. So the capital market has normally free funds available which can be used for capital export.

(c) Capital Export

The situation on the Swiss capital market made it possible to resume capital export in the form of public loans shortly after the end of the second World War. It started slowly, however, since most European countries did not yet have sufficient credit for borrowing on the open market. In the first few years Belgium was the principal country drawing on the Swiss market; as time passed other countries did the same. Since 1950 loans for foreign account developed as shown in Table 28.

Until the spring of 1969, bonds floated on the Swiss market for foreign account reached 9.1 billion francs. Thirty-three issues were in behalf of foreign

Table 28.

	Millions of francs		Millions of francs
1950	50	1960	660
1951	50	1961	1,012
1952	248	1962	705
1953	224	1963	589
1954	397	1964	386
1955	429	1965	339
1956	285	1966	561
1957	5	1967	898
1958	153	1968	1,089
1959	540	1969 (Jan.-Sept.)	703

[15] In the industrial sector internal financing as computed by deducting external financing from total real investment, is 5.6 billion (page 109). Computed as the sum of the sources of internal financing (depreciation-undistributed profits) 5.8 billion are obtained. A similar small difference can be found with respect to external financing of total investments. On the "uses" side we have 3.1 billion residential construction, 2.2 billion industry, and 1.8 billion public administration, which adds up to the 7.1 billion listed on page 110. The sum of the (external) sources, however, is 7.6 billion (page 110).

The differences, 0.2 billion in one case and 0.5 billion in the other, represent simply "statistical differences" in the sense in which this magnitude is usually entered in American "Sources and Uses of Funds" tabulations.

countries or cities. Belgium, including the Belgian Congo, went to the Swiss market eight times; Australia and Denmark, four times each; Norway three times; Japan, Sweden, and the cities of Oslo and Copenhagen, twice each. For the World Bank, loans totaling more than 900 million francs were raised between 1954 and 1968. Fifty-nine loans were floated in behalf of foreign banks and financial companies. Five of these issues were for International Standard Electric Corporation, three for Caltex Petroleum Corporation, and two for each of the following: Philips International Finance S.A., Luxemburg, Shell International Finance N.V., Montanunion, Bowater Corporation Ltd., Burlington International Inc. The Mortgage Bank of Vorarlberg (Austria) repeatedly tapped the Swiss market with minor issues; the Inter-American Development Bank raised two loans. More than 100 loans were raised in behalf of foreign industrial companies. The British Petroleum Corporation and the Lima Light and Power Company, Lima, Peru, each went to the Swiss market five times; Imperial Chemical Industries Limited (ICI), London, four times. Each of the following borrowed twice on the Swiss market: Pechiney Company, Petrofina S.A., N.V. Philips Gloeilampen, Telefonaktiebolaget L. M. Ericsson, and Saint-Gobain. Loans for power plants situated near the frontier, and for other foreign electric plants, were also floated repeatedly. Of the 230 foreign bonds recorded in the official list of the Zurich stock exchange, 209 were issued after the second World War. Foreign financial and holding companies such as Pirelli S.A., Basel, Dow Chemical A.G., Zurich, Eurofima, and others raised loans on the Swiss market the proceeds of which were invested abroad. There were eleven such firms; the total amount they borrowed was 940 million.

At the end of 1968, an amount of 7.64 billion of foreign loans was still outstanding. Adding the indirect capital export via foreign establishments in Switzerland, the total amount of capital involved was 8.6 billion francs. The geographical distribution of these loans is given in Table 29. It will be seen from the table that the EFTA countries participated with roughly 25%, the EEC countries with 30%, North and South America with 20%, the other countries with 7.5%, and international institutes with 17.5%, all percentages relating to capital exports in the form of bonds floated on the Swiss capital market. The most important debtor countries were as follows:

	Millions of francs
United States	1,486.6
Great Britain	1,157.0
German Federal Republic	836.0
France	668.1
Italy	429.0
Belgium	352.0

Table 29. Geographic Distribution of the Foreign Loans (In Millions of Swiss Francs)

Country	Foreign bonds	Loans via Swiss financial companies	Total
Great Britain	1157		1157
Denmark	200		200
Norway	277.2	30	307.2
Sweden	240		240
Austria	237		237
Portugal	24.6		24.6
Finland	46		46
EFTA	2181.8	30	2211.8
German Federal Republic	792	44	836
France	638.1	30	668.1
Italy	280	149	429
Belgium	352		352
Netherlands	302.5		302.5
EEC	2364.6	223	2587.6
Spain	40		40
Total Europe	4586.4	253	4839.4
USA	1196.6	290	1486.6
Canada	95		95
Mexico	50		50
Argentina	28		28
Peru	40.4		40.4
Total North and South America	1410	290	1700
South Africa	226.6		226.6
Japan	110		110
Australia	290		290
Total Rest of the World	626.6		626.6
World Bank	775		775
Inter-American Development Bank	110		110
Montanunion	80		80
Interfrigo	52		52
Eurofima		399	399
Total International Institutions	1017	399	1416
Grand Total	7640	942	8582

Table 30.

	Millions of francs		Millions of francs
1952	100	1961	414
1953	349	1962	211
1954	230	1963	206
1955	90	1964	196
1956	102	1965	153
1957	44	1966	484
1958	210	1967	1,265
1959	82	1968	1,243
1960	298		

In the years up to 1955 the interest rates on these loans average 4%. In the following years the average yield rose to 4½%; in the years 1964-65 it was 4¾%, and in 1967, 5.78%. In 1968 there was a minor reduction to 5.46%, but in 1969 interest rates from 5½ to 6¼% had to be offered. Despite this rise, the rates on the Swiss capital market were still markedly below those on other markets. The average yield of all loans is found to be 4.88% and the annual proceeds, 419 million francs.

At first the loans were subscribed, on the whole, by Swiss investors. Later the share of foreign subscribers rose to 30% and in the last few years to about 40%. With a view to the tight capital market the banks were sometimes advised to place 50% of the loans with their foreign clientele. However, owing to a special tax (Verrechnungssteuer), foreign customers do not seem to have been greatly interested in loans of foreign financial companies with branches in Switzerland. Assuming that 40% of the 7.6 billion loans raised in behalf of foreigners was subscribed by foreigners, the foreign participation would be 3 billion francs. Assuming 45%, we should arrive at 3.4 billion francs.

As well as the capital export in the form of public issues, there is the capital export by way of bank credits, security purchases, and direct investments. Since, according to Article 8 of the Banking Act, bank credits in excess of a certain amount and duration must be authorized by the National Bank, statistical information on such credits is available. It conveys the picture shown in Table 30.

In 1968 credits granted by the banks to foreign debtors (exclusive of money market investments) and still outstanding amounted to 8.9 billion francs. To this must be added credits to public agencies, mortgage investments, and participations in syndicates, in all 0.4 billion.

As a rule some 20 to 25% of the assets of the Swiss banks are deposited with

American and English banks in London, the center of the Euromoney market. Some 33% are in EEC countries, and almost 20% in the United States and Canada. The remainder is scattered in the other European countries and overseas.

Private capital export by security purchases is more difficult to estimate. It was probably subject to fairly heavy fluctuations from year to year, reflecting fluctuations on the stock exchange. Until fairly recently, security investments in the United States were in the foreground. Ever since the turn of the century, the American stock exchange has provided a rich assortment of investment possibilities, whereas in our own country only a limited market of shares existed. The unstable political conditions in Europe since 1914 made investments in the neighboring countries unattractive. So it could be assumed as late as the nineteen fifties that about one-half of all foreign security holdings represented American securities. But there was also lively interest in the shares of the great industrial companies of the Netherlands and in some French values. The high yield of the German bonds in the postwar period led to a certain reshuffling of investments. As a result earnings from Swiss investments in German securities today rank third after those from investments in United States and French securities. It should be added, however, that in the case of the German securities, the main emphasis is on bonds, whereas in the case of the other foreign securities, shares seem to be occupying the first place. Very recently the Eurobonds, especially the conversion loans, have met with considerable interest.

In the United States statistical records on purchases of American securities for foreign account are being kept. Swiss net purchases show the developments in Table 31.

On the Eurobond market, loans amounting to 1.8 billion dollars were issued in 1967. In 1968 the figure was 3.2 billion dollars. In 1966 the Swiss banks

Table 31.

	Millions of francs		Millions of francs
1951	259	1960	737
1952	256	1961	715
1953	406	1962	555
1954	460	1963	−60
1955	695	1964	−862
1956	1,090	1965	60
1957	543	1966	280
1958	258	1967	1,840
1959	1,363	1968	5,671

formed a syndicate for participation in such international issues. However, such loans were generally issued with a stamp that greatly restricts the possibility of such participations. So it is only very rarely that the banks can operate in the framework of the syndicate, which takes the foreign issue first as a fixed commitment. This limitation is in striking contrast to the vast potentialities of the Swiss banks for placing these Eurobonds. After all, according to the unanimous view of experts, 30 to 40% of the bonds issued on the Euromarket are being placed through the intermediary of the Swiss banks. For 1968 this would be in line with an amount of 1 to 1.2 billion dollars. Considering the American statistical data, and the loans in Swiss francs that are being raised in behalf of foreign debtors, we should have to estimate the total capital export effected through Swiss banks in 1969 at roughly 11 billion francs. Now it is obvious that such amounts could not have been raised for Swiss account only. Rather, the great achievement of the Swiss banks in placing securities must be explained by the fact that they administer large amounts of foreign property and that as a rule the earnings reaped from these assets as interest or dividends seek investment in securities. Moreover, the banks receive orders from their foreign customers to buy securities. What the figures reflect is the position of Switzerland as a financial center and the function of this center as a turning table.

How much of the purchases of foreign securities was for Swiss account has never been determined statistically and is difficult to estimate. At the end of the fifties, estimates of 150 to 200 million francs annually have been mentioned; this might easily have doubled in the course of the sixties. Assuming that only 10% of the American securities and Eurobonds purchased by the Swiss banks in 1968 were bought for Swiss account, we should arrive at something like 1 billion francs, but even this is probably too high.

As for the volume of Swiss portfolio holdings of foreign securities, in 1960 an estimate at 13 billion was ventured. In 1965 the estimate was 15.7 billion (including holdings in investment funds). But it was known that these were rather conservative approximations. In the meantime, figures contained in some recent agreements for the prevention of double taxation have become available, and the Commission for estimating the Swiss balance of payments on current account has refined the methods of estimation. On the basis of all available data from the double-taxation agreements, the material underlying the official estimate, and reports from banking quarters, we believe that it is defensible to come out with the figures shown in Table 32 (which are exclusive of loans in Swiss francs and direct investments).

By this reckoning, the holdings of foreign securities would be about 39 billion francs. To allow for possible sources of error, it seems reasonable to round the figure down to 35 billion. Again, the United States rank first with

Table 32.

Country or region	Income from capital millions of francs	Yield percent	Capital, millions of francs	Percent
United States	350	3 1/3	10,500	26
France	300	3 1/3	9,000	23
Germany				
Bonds	170	7		
Shares	80	3 1/3	4,800	12
Great Britain				
(including sterling				
area)	150	3 1/3	4,500	15
Netherlands	150	3 1/3	4,500	11
Austria and				
Scandinavian				
Countries	40	3 1/3	1,200	3
All Countries having				
agreement on double				
taxation	1,240		34,500	90
Rest of Europe	80	4	2,000	4
Central and South				
America	60	5	1,200	3
Canada, Japan,				
Australia, and				
rest of the world	60	5	1,200	3
Grand Total	1,440		38,900	100

26%, followed by France, Great Britain inclusive of the sterling area, and Germany. Within the sterling area, South Africa has a prominent place. In the Netherlands, Royal Dutch, 10% of whose capital is being administered by Swiss Banks, probably occupies the first place, followed by Unilever and Philips whose shares are quoted on the Zurich stock exchange. Concerning the yields data that underlie the estimates, it could be ascertained from records of the investment trusts that in 1968 the yield for stock was nearly everywhere slightly under 3%. To take account of the bonds with their higher rates of interest, a yield of 3 1/3% was chosen as the basis for the countries of Northern Europe and the United States, except that in the case of Germany a separate computation suggested itself because almost two thirds of the German securities here in question were bonds. For the other regions, yields of 4 to 5% were assumed. Even these estimates are bedeviled by a high degree of uncertainty, as there may be errors in either direction. It should be emphasized in particular that not all capital earnings are being accounted for on the basis of the double-taxation agreements. Nevertheless, we believe that the figures are defensible. The foreign securities are being held partly by investment trusts and partly by banks and financial companies. The banks and the financial companies show in their balance sheets foreign securities amounting to 1150 million francs, but the value of these securities as quoted on the stock exchange may well be close to 2.3 billion francs. The investment trusts, as will be shown later, administer foreign securities in an order of magnitude of 2.7 billion francs. Moreover it is reasonable to assume that the Swiss holding companies have at least 1000 million francs of foreign securities in their portfolios. So the amount held by all these agencies together may well be at least 6 billion francs. The value of all securities in the hands of private individuals or agencies may thus be assumed to amount to 29 billion francs.

To stimulate capital export, foreign stocks were quoted on Swiss stock exchanges. Thus we find 42 American and Canadian stocks quoted on the Zurich stock exchange. Among them are some of the best-known corporations, such as American Telephone and Telegraph Company, Baltimore and Ohio Railroad Company, Borroughs Corporation, Caterpillar Tractor Company, Chesapeake and Ohio Railway Company, Chrysler Corporation, Dow Chemical Company, E.I. DuPont de Nemours and Company, Eastman Kodak Company, Ford Motor Company, General Electric Company, General Foods Corporation, General Motors Corporation, IBM International Business Machines Corporation, International Telephone and Telegraph Corporation, Kennecott Corporation, Litton Industries, Inc., Mobil Oil Corporation, Montgomery Ward and Company, Inc., Procter and Gamble Company, Standard Oil Company of New Jersey, Union Carbide Corporation, F.W. Woolworth Company and so forth.

Among the 15 German stocks we find AEG-Telefunken, Badische Anilin-und Sodafabrik, J.P. Bemberg, Demag, DEGUSSA, Bayer, Hoechst, Mannesmann, Siemens, August Thyssen Huette, and the Volkswagenwerk. Among the 27 other foreign shares are the best-known Dutch international companies such as KZO, Philips, Royal Dutch, and Unilever. Among the English shares we find Bowater Paper and ICI, among the French ones we have Pechiney and Machines Bull. Belgium and Luxembourg are represented by Solvay, Sidro, Sodec, and others. Also, some South African and South American stocks are quoted in Zurich. Thanks to the more than 80 foreign stocks, Zurich has become one of the biggest European stock exchanges. Its volume of trade has reached the level of 3.7 billion francs per month.[16]

[16] In 1968 trade volumes on the European stock exchanges, expressed in billions of francs, were as follows: London 335.6, Zurich 41.5, Paris 26.1, Amsterdam 16.8, Milan 9.9, Frankfurt 7.9, Düsseldorf 7.9, Brussels 2.9, Madrid 1.8. It should be noted that in London and Zurich both purchases and sales are being counted, but on the German stock exchanges, only the purchases.

(d) The Role of the Bank for International Settlements (BIS)

The picture of the Swiss financial market would be incomplete without a reference to the Bank for International Settlements (BIS). This international financial agency was created in 1930. Its headquarters is in Basel. Its capital amounts to 500 million gold francs, one quarter of which has been paid in. In the spring of 1969 it was decided to double the capital, and the board of directors was authorized to issue another series of shares, amounting to 500 million francs, to be held exclusively by central banks. In this way the stock capital, which is largely in the nature of guarantee capital, can be raised to 1.5 billion gold francs.

At the beginning of its career the main task of the BIS was to function as a trustee in connection with the issue of the Dawes and Young loans. The war years brought most of the activities of the Bank to a standstill. The Bank was separated from its board of directors. Only the President of the Swiss National Bank was available, and he acted in those years as a trustee for his colleagues.

In the postwar period the Bank was assigned the important role of an agent to the European Payments Union, a task for which it was predestinated in every respect. The Bank fulfilled the task until 1958; later on it acted as agent of the European Currency Agreement.

In the main the activities of the BIS as a bank consist in taking in, as deposits, currency reserves—gold and foreign exchange—of the member countries, and in operating on the international gold market as buyer and seller. In its transactions, the BIS has to keep the policies of the participating central banks in mind.

Of special importance is the fact that the institute, in its monthly administration meetings, convenes the central bank governors of the most important countries, thus providing an opportunity for an exchange of opinions and for closer cooperation.

It was in the rooms of the BIS that the initial agreements on the cooperation of central banks were concluded—the "Basel Agreements" as they were later called. Subsequently the BIS became integrated more and more into the actions to aid individual central banks and today it plays a vital part in the measures designed to bolster the pound.

Since the BIS has its headquarters in Basel, it was natural that a close cooperation developed between this institute on one side and the Swiss National Bank as well as other Swiss banks on the other. Thus the BIS became attached to the American swapnet (pp. 55-59). Also the BIS plays an important role on the Swiss money market by taking in deposits from Swiss banks and investing the counterbalancing values on the international money markets. For some time now the BIS has been issuing so-called single bills of exchange on the Swiss market. These originated in connection with the reduction of the Swap obligations which the Federal Reserve Bank of New York had been handling. The American Treasury Department delivered to the BIS treasury bonds in Swiss francs (Roosa bonds); in return, the BIS delivered single bills of exchange to Swiss banks. At the end of 1968 the deposits of the Swiss banks with the BIS amounted to 470 million francs and the single bills of exchange were at the level of 1520 million francs. In this way the BIS has become a factor of some importance on the Swiss money market.

3. The Financial and Holding Companies

(a) The Financial Companies

The Swiss banking statistics lists 51 banklike financial companies, ten of which are in the business of taking in money deposits, whereas the others have no open access to the capital and money markets. At the end of 1968, the total capital of all financial companies amounted to 648.8 million francs. With reserves of 412.3 million francs, total available equity capital was 1061.1 million francs. Total assets stood at 2805.3 million. In the security portfolio, the aggregate value of which was 964.0 million francs, there were foreign securities amounting to 443.3 million (358.6 million stocks and 84.7 million bonds). For the most part these securities have been entered very conservatively; the actual value is probably higher by a significant margin. The companies had gross earnings totaling 135.0 million and net profits totaling 77.3 million, of which 59.0 million were being distributed. Earnings on securities made the biggest contribution (65.4 million). Interest margins yielded 15.4 million and commissions, 9.2 million.

The closeness of the ties between the Swiss financial companies and the economic world abroad is evident enough from the composition, mentioned above, of the 443 million francs security portfolio. Foreign banks probably account for a substantial portion of the 309.4 million francs "due from banks," and the same is true of the 863 million francs "due to banks." Foreign business may well account for 50%, or about 70 million, of the 135 million francs gross earnings.

A company of special character is the Eurofina A.G. in Basel. It was founded by the European railroads as an agency financing the purchase of rolling stock. Since 1957, the company has placed eleven loans on the Swiss market.

(b) The Holding Companies

According to the statistics of holding companies, at the end of 1968 there were 8353 holding companies with a capital of 9 billion francs. Of these, 1086 firms were classed as control and financing companies, 227 as investment companies, and 7040 as other holding companies. Taking capitalization as the criterion, the control and financing companies, with a capital of 7.2 billion, occupy first place. Development has progressed rapidly in the last ten years; as late as 1957 there were only 1992 holding companies with a capital of 1.8 billion francs.

The defense tax statistics lists, for the defense tax period 1963-64, 7661 companies under the comprehensive heading "Holding-Control-Patent Utilization." The companies were taxed on a taxable capital of 10.4 billion francs and a net profit of 1264 million francs. The seven world concerns with which we shall be dealing in Chapter 6 are not included here; they are classed as industrial enterprises. It is estimated that about 40% of the holding companies are Swiss controlled and 60% are foreign controlled, but it is sometimes difficult to be sure who stands behind such a company. For tax reasons, Swiss holding companies often assemble large and complex masses of private property under their control. Others are concerned with organizing a business concern in an economically rational manner. Still others are in their character close to real estate or financial companies.

As we have already noticed the number of foreign holding companies in Switzerland is large. In the postwar era it was mainly American concerns that set up Swiss holding or control companies in order to administer their European interests from there. The study of an American university on how best to administer the European interests of American business recommends gathering the European affiliated firms under the roof of one holding company. Some neutral country was recommended as headquarters for the company, and Switzerland was mentioned as particularly suitable because of her central location, her favorable traffic conditions, the fact that several languages are spoken there, and, last but not least, the convertibility of her currency. The tax advantages that holding companies enjoy in most cantons were emphasized in the second place only. The so-called holding privilege, to which attention may be drawn here, is based on the recognition that application of the full tax rates to a holding company would amount to double taxation of the same property and would make it impossible to set up such companies. For this reason all cantonal tax laws, as well as the law on the Federal defense tax, have set relatively low tax rates for holding companies. As these companies have great freedom in selecting the places of their headquarters, some cantons, such as Zug, Glarus, Graubuenden, and Freiburg, have adopted particularly low tax rates in order to attract holding companies.

Of the big American concerns that have organized holding companies in Switzerland, we name only the eight biggest: Caterpillar Tractor, DuPont de Nemours, Westinghouse, Chrysler, Dow Chemical, Procter and Gamble, Burroughs, and IBM. More than 1 billion francs is invested in these holding companies; they transfer annually about 400 million francs as dividends to their American parent corporations. We may infer from this that the affiliated companies represent a value of some 10 billion francs.

Extensive foreign interests are being administered also by the Société Financière Michelin, a holding company of the well-known French producer of tires, and by the Société Int. Pirelli S.A. in Basel. The latter company, which is affiliated to the Italian automobile tire concern, is not only a holding company, it is also a financial company. From 1956 to 1968 it has floated six loans on the Swiss market. Other companies that were active on the market are Viking S.A., Braun Electric International, Merck Holding, Renault Holding, Dow Chemical, Mobil Oil, Texaco, Conoco, and U.S. Rubber Overseas.

The Continental Linoleum Union in Zurich, which formerly had represented a peculiar form of combining the finances of European linoleum firms, has recently been transformed into a pure holding company. It controls numerous European producers of linoleum, and the former owners of the company have a controlling interest in it as shareholders.

So far the usefulness of foreign controlled holding companies for the Swiss economy as a whole has not been rated very high. These organizations were considered to be "transitory items" in Switzerland's international investment position and no item relating to their activities was entered in the Swiss balance of payments on current account. Today this view is no longer justified. In the defense tax period 1963-64 the foreign controlled holding companies paid defense taxes amounting to about 35 million francs. There were also payments of cantonal taxes that may well have amounted to 20 million. Total tax payments by these companies in 1964 may thus be estimated at roughly 55 million. Their other expenditures in Switzerland vary greatly. There are organizations that have a big administrative staff and laboratories forming part of their outfit, whereas others operate within the office of a lawyer or a trust company. On the average the expenditures are probably in the same order of magnitude as the tax payments, which means that the amount that should be entered in the balance of payments as income originating in these companies can be estimated at about 100 million francs for 1964. In the meantime these young companies have, in part, grown quite vigorously, and we may today estimate that about 180 million francs are being disbursed annually by these companies as taxes and expenditures. Frequently the international holding companies use the services of Swiss lawyers and trust firms. Compensation paid for these services may be estimated at 15 to 20 million francs. This, too, contributes to Switzerland's (current) balance of payments.

4. The Investment Trusts

The first investment trusts or investment funds were founded in 1860 in Scotland and somewhat later in England. In the United States the idea gained a foothold in 1918. In Switzerland the first trust funds of this type were set up in

1930 by the Société Internationale de Placement (SIP), a joint foundation of the Swiss Credit Bank and the Swiss Bank Corporation. At that time the main emphasis was on American and Canadian investments. The Union Bank of Switzerland founded a "Company for the administration of investment trusts," with headquarters in Zurich and Lausanne. In 1947 statistics recorded only 11 such funds. In 1955 there were 32 funds with property of 1.7 billion francs. The funds investing in securities had their bonanza time in the years 1958 to 1962. In those years the number of such funds rose from 20 to 63. Their market value reached a peak in 1961 with 3646 million francs. It declined to 2758 million francs in 1966, and then rose again. The funds investing in real estate experienced a vigorous upswing in the first half of the 1960s. From 1960 to 1965 their number rose from 44 to 179. Their market value culminated in 1963 with 3595 million francs. By 1967 it had declined to 3166 million. The total number of trust funds listed at the end of 1967 was 263, with investment property of 6668 million and a market value of 6256 million francs.

The rise and decline of the investment trusts is reflected most clearly in the number of shares in circulation: 5.8 million in 1955, 14.3 million in 1960, and 25.2 million in 1963, followed by a decrease to 21.9 million in 1967. The year 1968 marked a turning point. According to statistics compiled by the National Bank, 599 million francs of new money flowed into the funds in 1968, and 240 million could be set aside for redemption of shares. The total number of shares increased by 6.2 million in 1968 (in 1967 there still had been a decline), and the property of the funds surpassed the 7 billion mark once more. By mid-1969 it had gone up to 7.6 billion francs.

The statistics of the National Bank groups the investment trusts into funds investing in inland assets, funds investing in foreign assets, and mixed funds. At the end of 1968, 48 funds with inland investments were recorded. Four of them were investing in securities, and 44 had investments in real estate. The property of the funds with inland investments was 3.6 billion, of which 0.651 billion represented investment in securities. There were 16 funds investing in foreign assets, 12 in securities trust funds and 4 in real estate trust funds. It is in the funds investing in foreign securities that the retrograde development of the last few years shows most clearly. Whereas there were 17 such funds as late as 1967, there were only 12 at the close of 1968, with a property of 1576 million at the end of December. Of trust funds investing both in inland and foreign assets there were 39 at the end of 1968. Twenty-nine of them were securities funds, six were real estate funds, and four had investments in securities as well as in real estate. The property of this group amounted to 1.8 billion francs, 69 million of which represented real estate investments.

So long as security prices on the stock exchange were moving upward and real estate prices were rising year after year, the investment trusts did not encounter any serious problems. The situation changed for the securities trust funds after 1962 when security prices began to decline. For the real estate trust funds the change came after 1965, when the rise in real estate prices slowed down. Some securities funds that had not been administered too well, and some speculative real estate funds, ran into difficulties and had to be liquidated.

The necessity for Federal legislation on the investment trusts became apparent as early as the beginning of the sixties. On July 1, 1966, an act dealing with the subject went into effect. It contained rules on the legal nature of the investment funds, on the responsibilities of the management and the trustee, on investment policy, publicity, auditing, governmental supervision, and on liabilities. The act prescribes a specific distribution of the investment risks and forbids the pawning of assets. It makes it a duty of the funds to provide for an adequate degree of publicity and to use a uniform accounting schedule. The by-laws of the funds must clearly define the rights and duties of the parties involved. Auditing agencies and supervising authorities must keep a watchful eye on the business policy followed. According to an implementing regulation, advertisements for foreign investment trusts (which otherwise are not subject to Swiss law) require permission by the supervising authority. Supervision of the investment trusts was entrusted to the Federal Banking Commission.

Not all investment trusts were able to satisfy the requirements of the investment funds law. Those unwilling to abide by the provisions of the law had to dissolve or to adopt a different legal form of organization. By mid-1969, 129 Swiss funds had been placed under the law, and 52 foreign funds had obtained permission to advertise publicly in Switzerland.

The importance of the investment funds may be seen most clearly from a comparison with the other forms of saving. At the end of 1967, savings bank deposits amounted to 26.1 billion francs, deposits on passbooks to 7.5 billion, and demand deposits to 13.6 billion francs. This compares with 6 to 7 billion francs invested in certificates issued by investment funds. Saving through investment trusts has supplemented, in part even replaced, the forms of saving that had been in use previously. To prove that these other channels have suffered greatly because of the investment trusts would be difficult, however; after all, traditional saving via the banks increased by 11% in 1961 and by 10% in 1962—two years in which investment trusts were prospering; whereas in 1966, when investment trusts were on the downgrade, saving through other channels rose by only 7%.

The investment trusts could hardly have developed in Switzerland as vigorously as they did had it not been for the keen interest that the foreign customers of the Swiss banks took in this form of investment. Through the trust funds, the foreigners could invest without difficulty in Swiss real estate and in the Swiss joint-stock companies. Foreign participation in Swiss investment trusts is estimated by experts to be 40 to 50%.

124

Table 33.

Countries	Millions of francs	Percent
Great Britain	38.7	1.49
Denmark	0.8	0.03
Sweden	2.7	0.11
Austria	0.8	0.03
EFTA	43.0	1.66 ·
German Federal Republic	219.6	8.48
France	108.1	4.17
Italy	60.9	2.35
Belgium/Luxembourg	17.9	0.69
Netherlands	126.5	4.88
EEC	553.0	20.57
Spain	35.8	1.38
Europe	611.8	23.61
United States	1265.1	48.83
Canada	374.8	14.47
North America	1639.9	63.30
South Africa	290.4	11.21
Australia	14.3	0.55
Japan	32.1	1.24
International institutions (World Bank, Eurofina, etc.)	2.2	0.09
Sundry	339.0	13.09
Foreign assets end 1968	2590.7	100.00
Additions through mid-June 1969	170.0	
Foreign assets mid-1969	2760.7	

Some of the investment trusts with investments in foreign assets specialize in individual countries. The following funds record investments in the United States and Canada: AMCA America-Canada Trust Fund, "CANAC Anlagefond" fuer kanadische Aktien (Investment Fund for Canadian Shares), CANASEC Anlagefonds fuer kanadische Werte (Investment Company for Canadian Assets), USSEC Anlagefonds fuer amerikanische Werte (Investment Fund for American Assets). The Anglo-Valor Anlagefonds has assets of the British Commonwealth. The FRANCTT Fund specialized in French shares; the GERMANAC investment fund, in German shares; the ITAC in Italian shares; the ESPAC in Spanish shares; and the SAFIT, in South African assets. Three funds with both inland and

125

foreign investments have European assets. The holdings of some other funds are completely international; still others have concentrated on investments in particular lines of industrial or commercial activity.

On December 31, 1968, the values of the foreign investments of the more important Swiss investment trusts were distributed as follows:

The foreign investments of the funds, which for 1965 had been estimated at 2.7 billion and then temporarily declined to 2.2 billion, again attained the level of 2.7 billion francs at mid-1969.

The geographic distribution of the foreign assets of the investment funds at the end of 1968 can be seen from the table above, according to which the United States accounts for 49%, Canada for 14.5% and South Africa for 11.2%. Among the European countries, which account for 23.6% of all assets, West Germany ranks highest with 8.5%, followed by the Netherlands with 4.9% and by France with 4.2%. This means that the investment policy of the trust funds is markedly different from the policy followed by private investors. This may well be due to the fact that most of the funds started in the investment business in the postwar period and that some funds specialized on certain countries. The funds also make it a point to invest in securities that have large markets, and this explains the marked preponderance of American shares and the relatively high proportion of Dutch securities.

5. The Insurance Companies

In the course of the decades the Swiss insurance companies have built up, with many sacrifices and not without setbacks, an extensive foreign business. Even before the first World War, a few companies were active in Russia and other regions of what is now the East block, and they made efforts to get a foothold on the difficult American market. They have also since long been operating in the other European countries. Wars, crises, and inflation have destroyed much that had been built up by the work of many years. In World War II the internationally oriented companies were cut off from all their branch offices and affiliates, and after the end of the war they had to knit together again the threads that had been torn apart. Switzerland has 68 insurance companies, of which 18 are specializing in life insurance, 43 in accident and liability insurance, and 7 in reinsurance. Moreover 30 foreign companies are represented in Switzerland by branches; their business is keeping within narrow limits, however.

In the course of time, some of the Swiss companies have grown into organizations of world renown. The Schweizerische Rueckversicherungs-gesellschaft (Swiss Reinsurance Company), with an equity capital (including reserves) of 200 million francs and a concern capital of about 450 million francs

Table 34. Total Private Insurance Business of All Swiss Companies (in Millions of Francs)

	Gross premium payments[a]		Gross payments of benefits (including profit shares)		Capital investments[a]
	Total	Foreign (estimated)	Total	Foreign (estimated)	
1967	8,991	5,500	5,250	3,200	21,170
1966	8,565	5,300	5,055	3,100	19,523
1965	7,839	4,900	4,577	2,850	17,982
1964	7,178	4,500	4,191	2,600	16,576
1963	6,522	4,000	3,801	2,350	15,236
1962	5,986	3,700	3,370	2,100	14,258
1961	5,491	3,500	3,047	1,950	13,098
1960	5,057	3,200	2,782	1,750	12,103
1955	3,389	2,100	1,812	1,100	9,457
1950	2,170	1,300	1,179	700	6,447

[a]Sources: Eidgenoessisches Versicherungsamt, Jahresberichte über die privaten Versicherungsunternehmungen in der Schweiz.

is probably the largest organization of the world in this field of business. The concern as a whole received 2.1 billion francs as premiums in 1968-69. The company maintains ten branches and affiliated companies in the United States, Canada, South Africa, Australia, and Great Britain, as well as two consulting offices that are situated abroad. The "Zurich" Insurance Company with equity capital (including reserves) of 118 million, had revenues in 1968 in the form of premiums in the order of magnitude of 1.4 billion francs; the figure does not include the premiums paid to the affiliated companies. The parent corporation has 20 branches abroad and 18 affiliated companies in 23 countries. The Winterthur Accident Insurance Company, with equity capital (including reserves) of 120 million francs, received premiums amounting to some 760 million francs in 1968. It is represented in ten countries by branches, in six countries by affiliated companies, and in two countries by interests in other insurance companies. Moreover, the affiliated companies maintain branches in six other countries. And there are other insurance companies, such as the Helvetia group in St. Gallen and the Baloise group, that are represented abroad by affiliated companies and branches.

It will be seen from Table 34 that in 1950 total gross premium payments were 2170 million francs, of which 1300 million came from abroad, whereas in 1957 the total was 9 billion and the amount coming from abroad attained the level of 5.5 billion. Gross benefit payments, including profit shares, rose from 1.18 billion in 1950 to 5.3 billion in 1967. Of the latter amount, 3.2 billion went abroad. In the total foreign insurance business, reinsurance accounts for 3.3 billion, or 60%; the shares of accident and liability insurance and of life insurance in the total foreign business are 33% and 7%, respectively.

The premium income of the foreign subsidiary companies is not included in the available statistics. According to a statement by the Swiss Reinsurance Corporation it was 569 million francs in the business year 1968-69. The premium income of the largest accident insurance companies can be estimated at some 300 million francs.

In 1967 the insurance companies were administering funds amounting to slightly more than 21 billion francs, the share of the life insurance companies being 12.9 billion; that of the accident and liability insurance companies, 5.8 billion; and that of the reinsurance companies, 2.4 billion. Moreover, there were deposits of 2.5 billion. Capital investment abroad reached 6.4 billion francs at the end of 1967. Of this amount, 1.8 billion represented investment by the life insurance companies. Even this does not cover the totality of the foreign assets; on the basis of a questionnaire investigation into the five biggest companies this total was estimated to have been 6 billion francs at the end of 1965. Affiliated companies accounted for 560 million, short-term and medium-term investments for 1.9 billion, and long-term investments for the rest. In its Report to Stockholders for 1968-69 the Swiss Reinsurance Corporation stated that its total capital investment, much of which was investment abroad, amounted to some 3.5 billion (2.1 billion fixed investments and 1.4 billion short-term deposits). The capital represented by the concern as a whole, including the affiliated companies, amounts to 4.7 billion francs. The "Zurich" Insurance Company owns foreign bonds, valued at 1.17 billion francs, foreign real estate valued at 168 million, and stock valued at 395 million. The investments of the "Winterthur" Accident Insurance Corporation amount to 1.3 billion francs, 40% of which are foreign investments. Thus it turns out that the three companies just named account for almost 5 of the above-mentioned 6.4 billion francs in foreign investments. If the affiliated companies and the foreign interests are included in the count, the aggregate value of the foreign assets of the insurance companies may well be estimated to be 7.2 billion francs, offset by actuarial liabilities of roughly 5.8 billion francs. In these figures the capitals of the subsidiary companies are not included. The aggregate capital of the affiliated companies of the Swiss Reinsurance Company alone amounts to about 1.5 billion francs.

The importance of the Swiss insurance companies for the Swiss economy as a whole lies, among other things, in their contribution to the country's balance of payments. For 1967 this contribution has been estimated at 248 million francs. Expenditures in the social security sector, which in a sense offset that contribution, amounted to 8 million francs. In evaluating the contribution, account should be taken of the fact that in 1967 reinsurance was a loss business. The results of liability insurance were also unsatisfactory. In the case of the Swiss Reinsurance Corporation, the reinsurance business closed with a deficit of 42.6 million francs. The loss could be partially offset by a gain in life insurance, leaving a net loss of 23.6 million francs. Even the accident and liability insurance business closed with a technical loss of 135 million francs for all companies. Only the life insurance business yielded a satisfactory result. On examining the annual reports of the most important insurance companies one becomes convinced that the above-mentioned evaluation of the contribution of the insurance companies to the Swiss balance of payments may be regarded as conservative. If we take only the interest income earned on the foreign investments of the biggest insurance companies, we find that this income may well have amounted to more than 220 million francs. And the foreign accident and liability insurance business has partially offset the expenditures of the companies engaged in foreign business. To be sure, there is reason to think that in the last few years the companies doing foreign business would hardly have been able to pay dividends had it not been for the huge reserves that had been accumulated over the decades. However, taking the Swiss Reinsurance Corporation as an example, income from interest by far exceeded the actuarial losses from the insurance business proper. If in the next few years the reinsurance business remains unaffected by natural disasters such as hurricane Betsy, which caused 30 million francs damage, and if the liability insurance business becomes normalized by adjustment of the premiums, the contribution of the insurance companies to the balance of payments will in the future be more than 300 million francs annually. For the year 1968, 280 million could be entered in the statistics. In the annual business period 1968-69 the Swiss Reinsurance Corporation succeeded in offsetting losses from the accident and liability insurance business by a gain on life insurance. The result was a net profit of 0.6 billion francs.

With the possible exception of Great Britain, there is hardly a country in which the foreign sector of the insurance business accounts for so large a proportion of the total. In no small degree the Swiss insurance companies have to thank the neutrality policy and the monetary policy of the country for their impressive success in foreign business. In the anniversary pamphlet of the "Zurich" for the period 1872-1947 we read: "The monetary policy followed by the Confederation was of prime importance for Swiss insurance business. Had the leading authorities not displayed such a circumspect firmness in securing the stability of the country's currency, the reputation of Swiss insurance would certainly not have come out of the tests of the past years with flying colors, as it actually did. The companies are fully aware of this, and they are grateful for it."

129

6. The Big Industrial Concerns

For the developing Swiss industry of the nineteenth century, tariff barriers and transportation costs were an obstacle that often was difficult to conquer. So the idea of overcoming the narrowness of the home market by setting up establishments abroad gradually ripened. The accession of Baden to the German Customs Union in 1836 induced a few firms to build plants on the other side of the Rhine. At that time it was mostly entrepreneurs in the textile field who ventured into such expansions; it is noteworthy that 39 of the 56 Swiss textile establishments in Germany had their origin before 1900. As early as 1874, the joint-stock company Arthur Rieter set up an establishment in Konstanz. In 1895 the Georg Fischer A.G. in Schaffhausen followed with an affiliated establishment in Singen. Likewise still in the past century, the Nestlé A.G. in Vevey and the Anglo-Swiss Condensed Milk Company in Cham, the two founding firms of the present Nestlé Alimentana A.G. organized affiliated companies abroad. So did the Maggi Company, which today belongs to the Nestlé group. In 1897 the company established an affiliate in Singen. For the chemical industry, which was centered in Basel, it was natural to build establishments across the frontier, in Loerrach, Grenzach, Wehr, and Waldshut. Originally, these establishments were often merely affiliated plants, and even today some of them are operating as subsidiary plants lacking legal status.

The various foreign interests of Swiss industry are numerous and difficult to keep track of. Nearly every major enterprise has establishments abroad, be it in one of the neighboring countries or overseas. But only a few have built up a network of subsidiary companies that constitutes a world-wide concern. These concerns are Nestlé Alimentana A.G. in Cham and Vevey, F. Hoffmann-La Roche and Company A.G., Ciba A.G., J. R. Geigy A.G., Sandoz A.G.—all four in Basel; Aktiengesellschaft Brown, Boveri and Company in Baden, and Schweizerische Aluminium A.G. in Chippis-Zurich. We shall be dealing with the last-named concerns in more detail below. These seven firms probably account for about two thirds of all Swiss direct investments abroad. But it should not be overlooked that other big firms, such as Gebr. Sulzer A.G. in Winterthur, Escher Wyss and Company (closely associated with the Sulzer firm), Georg Fischer A.G. in Schaffhausen, and Landis and Gyr A.G. in Zug, have substantial investments abroad. The same holds for C. F. Bally A.G. and for the interests of the Schindler group which have been knit together in the Schindler Holding A.G. In the cement industry the Holderbank controls a substantial foreign business domain.

The largest network of affiliated companies, the one with the widest ramifications, has been organized by the Nestlé Alimentana A.G. To name only its most important transactions, the corporation has taken over the Maggi

Table 35. Balance Sheets of Five Concerns, December 31, 1968 (In millions of Francs)

	Alusuisse	Ciba	Geigy	Sandoz	Nestlé	Total
Assets						
Plant						
Machinery	1,496.1	1,539.0	1,876	1,176.4	1,911	7,998.5
Equipment						
Furniture						
Financial interests	154.6	120.0	159	80.8		514.4
Other assets					302	302.0
Sundry fixed items	17.4					17.4
Alusuisse shares deposited as collateral for conversion loan	30.0					30.0
Total fixed assets	1,698.1	1,659.0	2,035	1,257.2	2,213	8,862.3
Inventories	469.5	940.1	801	424.9	2,182	4,817.5
Current loans	424.4	641.0	546	496.6	1,089	3,197.0
Liquid assets	310.8	414.2	441	376.4	1,373	2,915.4;
Total circulating assets	1,204.7	1,995.3	1,788	1,297.9	4,644	10,929.9
Total Assets	2,902.8	3,654.3	3,823	2,555.1	6,857	19,792.2
Liabilities						
Stock capital	250.0 ⎫			130.0	196	(Nestlé)
Reserves	298.0 ⎬ 2,490.9		2,832	1,402.0	100	(Unilac)
Consolidation reserve	950.7 ⎭				992	(Nestlé)
Special reserves				247.5	267	(Unilac)
Other equity capital (incl. reserves of affiliated and allied companies for renewal of fixed assets)					456	
					2,691	
Total equity capital	1,498.7	2,490.9	2,832	1,779.5	4,702	13,303.l
Long-term debts	801.5	366.0	262	158.1	603	2,190.6
Short-term debts	555.3	797.4	729	583.1	1,552	4,216.8
Financial interests of outsiders				34.4		34.4
Profit and loss account	47.3					47.3
Total debt capital	1,404.1	1,163.4	991	¹775.6	2,155	6,489.1
Total liabilities	2,902.8	3,654.3	3,823	2,555.1	6,857	19,792.2

Alimentana A.G. in Kempthal and the Crosse and Blackwell in England, and it has for some time been controlling the Findus Company. Besides its old basic products, condensed milk and foodstuffs for children, the Nestlé group today manufactures chocolate, food products of all kinds, instant beverages such as the familiar Nescafé, and deep-freeze products. In its Annual Report for 1968 Nestlé put the insurance value of its plant and equipment at 4.2 billion francs. Keeping in mind the structure of the concern, it is safe to assume that 90% of this plant and equipment is situated abroad. For financial interests and loans to subsidiary companies, 1.9 billion francs have been entered in the balance sheet.

In machinery industry, the joint-stock company Brown, Boveri and Company, Baden, has grown into a world concern. Its biggest affiliated company is the Brown, Bovery and Company A.G. in Mannheim, with 100 million deutschmark stock capital, 56% of which is owned by the parent company, and a turnover of 1454 million deutschmarks in 1968. With 36,000 employees, the Mannheim subsidiary has outranked the parent company. Fixed and circulating assets of the Mannheim firm amount to 956 million German marks. The firm is probably the biggest affiliated company that has so far been set up by any Swiss enterprise. The French subsidiary, the Compagnie Electro-Mécanique in Paris, takes second place with a stock capital of 35 million French francs. In 1967 the number of employees was 8756; the turnover reached 640 million francs. Other subsidiary companies are operating in Italy, Norway, Austria, the Netherlands, Belgium, Spain, Canada, and the United States.

Of outstanding importance are the foreign interests of the four Basel concerns belonging to the chemical industry, Hoffmann-La Roche, Ciba, Geigy, and Sandoz. Ciba, Geigy, and Sandoz had their origins in the chemistry of dyestuffs, later they extended their activities to pharmaceutical chemistry, agrochemistry, and products such as glues, varnish, chemical building materials, plastics, and so on. By contrast, Hoffmann-La Roche has concentrated on pharmacochemistry right from the start, and is today probably the world's biggest enterprise in this field. Only later did the company expand its production program.

In the interwar period the financial interests of Ciba, Geigy, and Sandoz were running parallel in many respects. So the three companies established a community of interests. This provided an opportunity for setting up, in foreign countries, subsidiaries representing joint ventures of the three Swiss firms. Subsidiaries organized and kept operating on this basis were the Clayton Aniline Company Ltd. at Clayton near Manchester, England, the Societa Bergamasca per l'Industria Chimica at Seriate near Bergamo, Italy (this firm, however, was liquidated in 1968), and the Toms River Chemical Corporation in Toms River, U.S.A. Ciba, Sandoz, and the firm of Wander (Bern) united in founding a subsidiary in Egypt; Ciba and Wander jointly organized an affiliated firm in Istanbul. In Resende, Brazil, there is a firm in which Ciba, Sandoz, and Geigy have financial interests. Recently the community of interests of the three Basel firms has been dissolved and each of them is developing in its own way. But all three have become large-scale concerns of world importance. In the spring of 1969, Ciba and Geigy announced that they would examine the possibilities of a closer cooperation and at the end of 1970 the two concerns merged.

The seventh big Swiss concern is the Schweizerische Aluminium A.G., or Alusuisse, for short, which is active in all phases of aluminum production and processing. The firm is one of the six biggest aluminum producers of the world. It also owns raw materials, plants, power plants, and factories manufacturing electrodes; for some time it has been branching out into the artificial chemical material field. At present the company is about to organize a major industrial establishment in the United States on the Gulf Coast and—jointly with an Australian minority group—a raw materials plant in Australia. With 1.5 billion francs invested in it, the last-named plant will be by far the biggest investment in the history of the Swiss corporation. It may well be the most important raw materials basis of the concern for decades to come. Also, an aluminum rolling mill is about to be set up in Iceland, based on the water power that is available there.

At the end of 1968 the seven big Swiss concerns named above were employing some 300,000 persons in all, 50,000 of them in Switzerland. Thus, measuring by the number of workers, five sixths of the total are situated in foreign countries. Altogether, the seven concerns had a turnover of 25.4 billion francs and the recorded equity capital of the parent companies, including reserves, amounted to 4.5 billion francs. This figure does not tell us very much, however, since one of the biggest of the seven, the Hoffmann-La Roche, has paid back the stock capital and is working, on the whole, with open and latent reserves. More informative are the statements of four of the firms on the insurance value of their plant and equipment. The reported amount was more than 9 billion francs. In its report for 1967, which has recently been granted an award for the frankness and the detailed information it provided, Alusuisse set the value of the fixed assets of the companies forming the concern at 2424 million, of which 1.4 billion have been written off. The value of the minority interests was 148 million francs (see Table 38).

Partly on the basis of information furnished by the firms, the author of this book has estimated the foreign assets of the seven big concerns at 12 billion francs at the end of 1965. This amounts to 65% of all Swiss direct investments, which later have been estimated at 17.5 billion at the time point just indicated. Numerous minor and scattered investments could not be covered in deriving these estimates. Since the end of 1965, direct investments have risen further. On their development in the case of four companies we have the figures shown on page 134.

Alusuisse estimates its investments at 209 million francs for 1967 and 233

	1964	1965	1966	1967	1968
		(Millions of francs)			
Nestlé	295	345	376	366	353
Geigy	270	291	250	300	342
Ciba	221	240	229	239	216
Sandoz	155	170	230	280	240
Total	941	1,046	1,085	1,185	1,151

million for 1968. In the average of the years 1964 to 1966, the investments of the company amounted to 270 million. A third source of information estimates the investments of Hoffmann-La Roche at 300 million francs and those of the Brown, Boveri concern at 290 million, both for the year 1967. With respect to all seven concerns we thus arrive at a total investment of 1980 million francs for the year 1967.

Geigy states that in 1967, 76% of its investments were investments in foreign assets. In the case of Ciba the proportion was 55% and in the case of Sandoz, about 60%. We may therefore assume that from 1964 to 1967 the annual foreign investments of the seven big concerns have risen from about 1.1 to 1.4 billion francs. From 1965 to the end of 1968, 4 billion may well have been invested abroad. The foreign assets of the seven big concerns, which we have estimated at 12 billion francs in 1965 have probably risen to between 18 and 19 billion by the end of 1968.

Concerning the geographical distribution of the investments, Geigy in its annual Report for 1968 tells us that 51% of the company's investments went to North America, most of it to the United States, 7% to EEC countries, 40% to EFTA countries (of which 32% went to Switzerland), and 2% to others. The heavy preponderance of investments in the United States is explained by the fact that Geigy is about to build near Baton Rouge (St. Gabriel) on the Mississippi a big plant covering an area of eight square kilometers for production of agricultural and industrial chemicals, and at the same time it is organizing the McIntosh factory (in Alabama). Alusuisse informs us that of its 1968 investments the EEC countries took 64%, the EFTA countries, including Switzerland, 12%, and the other countries, primarily the United States, 24%. From the Annual Report of Nestlé we can gather that in 1967 more than 28 million francs were invested in France, more than 17 million in England, 15 million in Spain, 13 million in Italy, 24 million in the United States, 7.4 million in South Africa, and 7.5 million in Switzerland. But these are only a few examples. The total operating expenditures of Geigy were regionally distributed as follows at the end of 1968: EFTA 45% (Switzerland 35%); North America, 30%; EEC, 17%; Latin America, 4%; other regions, 4%.

In the case of Hoffmann-La Roche, as in the case of Geigy, the United States ranks highest in the regional distribution of the concern's foreign investments whereas Alusuisse and Brown-Boveri are strongly oriented towards EEC. The concern transactions of Ciba and Sandoz warrant the conclusion that their investments in the United States must likewise be quite substantial. This can be inferred from the fact that the proportion of their turnover in that country was 25% and 29%, respectively, of their total turnover. In the case of Nestlé the dispersion of interests is wider. About 30% of all factories are in EEC countries, 19% in EFTA countries, 24% in Latin America, and only 8% in North America.

About the financing of these huge investments we find scattered information in a few company reports. Thus Nestlé states that in 1968 the two holding companies made available 150 million francs for such purposes, while 99 million were financed out of reserves and 51 million came from undistributed profits. Geigy tells us that the whole investment of 342 million francs was financed from internal sources. The same was true in the case of Hoffmann-La Roche; in fact, this company has never tapped the capital market in the last 40 years. Sandoz, which in 1967 invested 280 million francs, reported a cash flow of 250 million, of which 30 million were distributed. There was thus a financing gap of 60 million francs; it was closed by issuing shares for 20 million francs and by drawing on the liquid assets of the parent company. In the case of Ciba, too, the investments are being financed out of internal sources. Alusuisse, in its Annual Report for 1968, referring to the concern as a whole, states that 388 million francs were financed internally and 101 million externally. Applying these proportions to the investments, it would appear that 80% of them were financed from internal and 20% from external sources.

Of particular interest is the financing of the industrial aggregate which Alusuisse is about to organize on the Gulf Coast of the United States. The investment is financed by the parish Calcasieu, which is leasing out the whole plant to an affiliated company of Alusuisse. When the costs of the investment are repaid, the plant will become the property of the subsidiary company. What we have here is a large-scale leasing operation of a type which is no longer permissible under American law. As for the big Alusuisse investment in Australia, part of the financing was done by a Euro conversion loan of 60 million dollars, issued not long ago by a financial subsidiary of Alusuisse. More than one half of this loan was probably subscribed by Swiss and foreign customers of Swiss banks.

As a new feature, five big concerns, Alusuisse, Nestlé, Ciba, Geigy, and Sandoz, publish consolidated balance sheets covering their concerns comprehensively. The balance sheets have been brought together in Table 35.

As will be seen from the table, total fixed assets of the five firms amount to 8.9 billion francs, total circulating assets are 10.9 billion francs, total debt capital is 6.5 billion francs, and total equity capacity is 13.3 billion francs. In the case of Nestlé, the proportion of circulating in relation to fixed assets is striking. This may be partly due to the fact that in the food industry investments are relatively lower than in the chemical and metallurgical industries. There is also reason to assume that in the case of Nestlé a higher proportion of the existing plant and durable equipment has been written off than in the case of other concerns; as a matter of fact, with Nestlé the insurance values of these fixed assets are more than double the values recorded in the balance sheet.

The amount of latent reserves is difficult to ascertain. They are hidden in depreciation charges to the extent that these exceeded what was required to offset physical wear and tear as well as obsolescence. In this connection we may note that the item "Plant, Machinery, Equipment, Furniture," amounting to 8 billion francs, is not much higher than the new investments of the last six years, and that it falls short of the insurance value by 2.8 billion francs. Moreover, there is real estate, estimated by Sandoz to extend over 192 hectares. Since part of this lies within the territory of Basel City, the real estate owned by the five firms probably represented a substantial value. Considering all this, the latent reserves lying in the fixed assets may well be estimated at more than 3 billion. Inventories, with 4.8 billion, and Current Loans, with 3.2 billion, are rather low, considering that the turnover is about 18 billion francs. On the other hand, Liquid Assets, with 2.9 billion francs, are fairly high; they offset roughly 70% of the short-term liabilities.

In the case of Brown, Boveri, construction of a consolidated balance sheet is difficult because, as a rule, only slightly more than 50% of the shares of an affiliated firm are owned by the parent company. As for Hoffmann-La Roche, the item "Other Equity Capital," whose composition would probably be similar to that of the same item with Nestlé, would be taking the place of "Stock Capital," since this latter has been repaid. There would hardly be any long-term debts. Short-term debts would be relatively low in relation to the turnover. The same would probably be true of the inventories, which would be lower than the current loans, whereas the liquid assets might well exceed even those of Nestlé.

So far, only Alusuisse and Nestlé have published consolidated income statements. Nestlé in 1968 had 8478 million gross sales, 5509 million cost of fabrication, and 2262 million selling expenses and losses from financial margins. The result was a gross profit of 707 million francs reduced by taxes to 405 million. Now, Nestlé in 1968 distributed 121 million, and invested 353 million francs; these two items together took 474 million francs. It must therefore be inferred that the cost items include depreciation allowances to the tune of 69 million francs—unless some affiliated companies have drawn on external sources to finance their investments. In the case of Alusuisse a consolidated net profit of 96.8 million resulted after depreciation allowances of 141 million francs. Since investments amounted to 233 million francs, and the distribution of profits took 31.6 million, the financing of the investments required an additional amount of

Table 36. The Swiss Big Concerns in the World[a]

	Nestlé	Hoffmann-La Roche	Ciba	Sandoz Wander	Geigy	Brown Boveri Oer-likon	Alussuisse
Total F & G	78 (C)	65 (F)	65 (F)	87 (F)	37 (F)	21 (F)	55 (E)
	208 (E)		6 (J)	7 (J)	8 (J)		44 (J)
Switzerland	1 (C)	4 (F)	5 (F)	2 (H)	1 (H)	4 (F)	18 (F)
	4 (E)		3 (J)	6 (F)	2 (F)		
				3 (J)	4 (J)		
Europe							
Great Britain							
Ireland	2 (C)	1 (F)	1 (H)	4 (F)	1 (F)		3 (F)
	19 (E)		6 (F)	1 (W)			
Germany	1 (C)	1 (F)	1 (F)	2 (F)	3 (F)	1 (F)	10 (F)
	10 (F)			1 (W)			3 (I)
France	1 (C)		3 (F)	3 (F)	5 (F)	1 (F)	2 (F)
	28 (E)			2 (W)		1 (0)	
Italy	1 (C)	1 (F)	2 (F)	1 (F)	1 (F)	1 (F)	2 (F)
	12 (E)			1 (W)			3 (I)
Austria	1 (C)	1 (F)	1 (F)	6 (F)	1 (F)	1 (F)	1 (F)
	3 (E)			1 (W)			
Belgium	1 (C)	1 (F)	1 (F)	1 (F)	1 (F)	1 (I)	1 (F)
	3 (E)			2 (W)		1 (O)	
Netherlands	1 (C)	1 (F)	1 (F)	1 (F)	1 (F)	1 (I)	2(F)
	11 (E)						1 (I)
Denmark	1 (C)		1 (F)	1 (F)			
	6 (E)						
Sweden	1 (C)	1 (F)	1 (F)	1 (F)	1 (F)		
	3 (E)						
Norway	1 (C)					1 (I)	1 (F)
	4 (E)						
Finland				1 (F)			
Spain	1 (C)	1 (F)	1 (F)	3 (F)	3 (F)	1 (I)	
	11 (E)			1 (W)		1 (O)	
Portugal	1 (C)		1 (F)	2 (F)			
	1 (E)			1 (W)			
			Dr. A. Wander-Ciba SA, Istanbul				
Iceland							1 (F)
Turkey	1 (C)	1 (F)		2 (F)			
	1 (E)			1 (W)			
Greece				1 (F)	1 (F)		
North America							
United States	1 (C)	2 (F)	1 (H)	1 (F)	1 (F)	1 (F)	2 (F)
	15 (E)		4 (F)	1 (W)			
			Toms River Chemical Corp., Toms River				
Canada	1 (E)	2 (F)	1 (F)	3 (F)	1 (F)	1 (F)	
				1 (W)			

137

Table 36 continued

	Nestlé	Hoffmann-La Roche	Ciba	Sandoz Wander	Geigy	Brown Boveri Oerlikon	Alussuisse
Asia							
India	1 (C) 2 (E)	1 (F)	2 (F)	1 (F) 1 (W)	2 (F)	1 (F)	
Japan	1 (C) 2 (E)	1 (F)	1 (F) 1 (I)	2 (F)	2 (F)		
Hongkong	1 (C)	1 (F)	1 (F)	1 (F)	1 (F)		
Philippines	1 (C) 1 (E)	1 (F)		1 (F) 1 (W)			
Rest of Asia	9 (C) 2 (E) (Malaysia)		1 (F) (Pakistan)	1 (F) (Pakistan) 1 (W) (Singapore)	1(F) (Pakistan)		
Australia and							
New Zealand							
Australia	7 (E)	1 (F)	1 (F)	1 (H) 1 (F) 1 (W)	1 (F)		1 (F)
New Zealand	2 (E)		1 (F)	1 (F) 1 (W)			
Central and							
South America							
Mexico	1 (C) 6 (E)	2 (F)	2 (F)	2 (F) 1 (W)	1 (F)	1 (J)	
Brazil	1 (C) 10 (E)	2 (F)	1 (F) Industrias Quimicas Resende SA, Resende	1 (F) 1 (W)	3 (F)	1 (J) 1 (O)	2 (F)
Argentina	1 (C) 5 (E)	2 (F)	1 (F)	1 (F) 1 (W)	2 (F)	1 (F)	
Chile	1 (C) 6 (E)		1 (F)	2 (F)	1 (F)		
Venezuela	5 (E)	1 (F)	1 (F)	1 (F) 1 (W)			
Colombia	7 (E)	2 (F)	1 (F)	1 (F) 1 (W)			
Uruguay		1 (F)	1 (F)	1 (F)			
Peru	2 (E)	1 (F)	1 (F)	1 (F)		1 (F)	
Cuba				1 (F)			
Jamaica	2 (E)	1 (F) for the whole region		1 (W)			
Guatemala	1 (E)						
Panama	1 (E)						
Puerto Rico	1 (E)						
Trinidad	1 (E)						

	Nestlé	Hoffmann-La Roche	Ciba	Sandoz Wander	Geigy	Brown Boveri Oerlikon	Alussuisse
Rest of Central and South America	15 (C)						
Africa							
South Africa	1 (C) 9 (E)	2 (F)	1 (F)		2 (F)	1 (J) 1 (O)	
Egypt				Swisspharma, SAA, Cairo			
Ivory Coast	1 (E)						
Kenya	1 (E)						
Nigeria	1 (C) 1 (E)						2 (F)
Rhodesia	1 (C) 1 (E)						
Kenya-Uganda-Tanzania			1 (F)				
Morocco							
Tunisia	1 (C) 1 (E)			1 (F)			
Guinea							1 (I)
Sierra Leone							1 (F)
Rest of Africa	10 (C)						

[a]Abbreviations:

C Administrative center
E Affiliated establishment (organized for production)
F Affiliated firm (parent company's interest less than 50%)
H Holding company
J Joint enterprise (organized by several parent companies)
W Wander
O Machinery factory Oerlikon

about 30 million francs. This requirement could be amply met by an increase of capital (150 million) and by an increase of short-term debts (101 million).

If, in analogy with Nestlé, we were to estimate the consolidated gain on the basis of distributed profits plus 80% of new investments, we would arrive, for Ciba, Geigy, and Sandoz taken together, at a consolidated profit in the order of magnitude of perhaps 740 million francs. On the basis of stock exchange valuations, comparing them with those relating to Nestlé, we could arrive at a consolidated profit (before depreciation) of 750 million francs. As for Hoffmann-La Roche, the stock exchange which estimates the intrinsic value of the firm at almost double the value of Nestlé obviously surmises that the consolidated profit of Hoffmann-La Roche is in an order of magnitude of more than 700 million francs. This does not seem impossible, considering that the sale of pharmaceuticals usually yields high profit margins and that the turnover of the concern is 3.5 billion francs. So the consolidated concern profits (before depreciation) of the six big concerns (Brown, Boveri being left out) can be estimated at about 2 billion francs.

The methods used in organizing the foreign direct investments vary greatly from concern to concern. Nestlé and the four chemical firms generally make it a point to exercise full control over their subsidiary companies. By contrast, the policy of Brown, Boveri was to let financial quarters of foreign countries become interested in its own affiliated companies. Alusuisse mentions 55 firms as being controlled by it, and 44 financial interests of less than 50%. These findings about the policies of the various concerns are not without exceptions. Thus Nestlé in 1968 had (only) an 80% control over the Findus group; until 1969, even its control over Sarotti was only a majority interest. There is little information about the financial interests of the chemical industry. It is known, however, that Hoffmann-La Roche has taken over the Geneva concern Givaudan (in the field of aromatic and spicy articles), that it controls the Sauter S.A. in Geneva and the Panteen A.G. in Basel, and that it has recently taken a 25% interest in the Société Genevoise d'Instruments de Physique (SIP). Ciba was interested, jointly with ICI, in the photographic firm Ilford; in November, 1969, it took over the ICI share, too. Ciba also controls the Zyma S.A. in Nyon. Sandoz, in 1967, took over the Dr. Wander A.G. in Bern, which brought numerous foreign investments into the Sandoz concern. Recently, Durand and Huguenin has merged with Sandoz. By the fact that Sandoz acquired an interest in the Internationale Verbandstoff-Fabrik Schaffhausen, the diversification of its interests has for the first time branched out into nonchemical territory.

In the structure of the Nestlé and Hoffmann-La Roche concerns there is a similarity inasmuch as both firms have organized parallel holding companies. The shares of these companies are "chained" to those of the parent companies, so that the same shareholders are represented in both. In the case of Nestlé the parallel holding company Unilac Inc. in Panama administers the interests of the concern in the Western hemisphere, except for the United States, and in the Pacific. In the case of Hoffmann-La Roche, the parent company controls the firms in continental Europe and in the Middle East, while the parallel holding company Sapac Corporation in Saint John (Canada) is in charge of the establishments in North and Latin America, in the sterling area, in the Pacific regions, and in the Far East. Thus, in this case, the parallel holding company has been given an even wider scope of activity than in the case of Nestlé.

The Nestlé firm is itself organized as a holding company, whereas in the case of Hoffmann-La Roche the parent company does its own producing and exporting. As for the other chemical concerns, the subsidiary firms are directly

140

owned by the parent companies which are themselves active in manufacturing and exporting. In recent times Geigy and Sandoz have each assembled the foreign subsidiary firms in a holding that is itself an affiliate of the parent company. Ciba has grouped its subsidiaries in England and in the United States under the roofs of holding companies.

While the Hoffmann-La Roche concern does not publish any details in its annual reports, it is known to control at least 22 chemical factories, 35 establishments manufacturing finished pharmaceutical articles, and 120 selling agencies. The most important of these latter are in Nutley (U.S.A.) with 6000 to 7000 workers, in Grenzach (Germany) with 1700, and in England with 1000 workers. The Nestlé concern maintains in most countries special administrative centers whose job it is to look after the factories and sales organizations established there. In 40 countries, the concern has set up 78 administrative centers, 208 factories, and 536 sales agencies. It thus dominates a truly world-wide organization. Ciba controls 65 manufacturing and sales firms. Sandoz, which in 1967 took over the Dr. Wander in Bern, has today some 87 subsidiary companies, 26 of which were brought in by the Dr. Wander firms. Geigy lists 37 important affiliated companies in its Annual Report. Brown, Boveri reports 21 subsidiary firms and interests. Alusuisse controls 55 companies and is interested in 44 others. In its Annual Report the names of 64 such companies have been mentioned.

Thus, as far as can be ascertained from publications, all seven concerns taken together maintain about 650 affiliated companies, or financial interests, or manufacturing establishments. Nine subsidiaries are operating as joint ventures—four of them as Swiss and five as foreign enterprises—of several parent companies. About 40 subsidiaries are established in Switzerland. And these data are by no means complete. Nestlé and Hoffmann-La Roche together maintain 656 sales agencies all over the world.

Table 37 gives information on the geographic distribution of the affiliated organizations. The table should not be regarded as fully comprehensive, however, as some firms report only on the most important subsidiaries.

The primary contribution that direct investments abroad are making to the economy of the homeland is the opening of market areas that cannot be reached directly by the parent companies. The proceeds from these sales are reflected in the profit distributions of the affiliated firms. In the 1967 income statements of the six concerns that are not organized as holding companies, these distributed profits amount to 168 million francs, of which some 140 million probably originated abroad. Now, whereas this is a sizable sum, it is not in any reasonable proportion to the huge investments in the foreign countries. In the case of the Nestlé concern, which is organized as a holding company, the revenues of the affiliated companies naturally are the main source of income. From the report for the year 1968 we can gather that the affiliated and associated companies

Table 37 Swiss Big Concerns 1968 (Millions of Francs)

	Nestlé (Unilac)	Hoffmann-La Roche (Sapac)	Ciba	Geigy	Sandoz Wander	Brown Boveri	Alusuisse
Employees (concern)	90,075	24,000(E)	30,746	23,961	25,670	88,100	23,757
Employees (Switzerland or parent company)	4,000(E)	4,000(E)	9,310	6,681	6,865	15,882	3,686
Turnover (concern)	8,478	3,500(E)	2,655	2,730	2,194	4,018	1,775
Equity capital (including reserves of parent company)	1,155 (N) 332 (U)	b	566	591	541	780	587
Insurance value of fixed assets	4,160	424 (Basel)	2,089 (1967)	1,928	1,157	1,156	1,500(E)
Total assets	564(N) 396(U)	614(H) 207(S)	1,202	1,010	1,098		740
Number of affiliated firms, financial interests, plants	78(C) 208(P)	65(E)	65	37	87	21	55(F) 44(I)
Annual investments	353	350(E)	216	342	240	290(E)	233
Stated net profits	132(N)a 40(U)	50(H) 40(E)	47	31.7	43	20	32c
Research expenditures		233	233		176		
Capitalization by stock exchange (Mid-1969)	5,125	10,520	3,855	4,385	2,831	946	1,552

aConsolidated net profit 405. bStock capital paid back. cConsolidated net profit 97. dAbbreviations: C, administrative center; E, estimate; F, affiliated firm; I, financial interest of parent company; N, Nestlé, U, Unilac, H, Hoffmann-La Roche, S, Sapag.

contributed 339 million francs, of which they retained 56 million for their own investments. The remaining 283 million, plus 20 million interest on short-term investments, gave 303 million francs gross income. Taxes and expenditures amounted to 32 million, leaving a net income of 271 million francs. Of these, 99 million were reserved. The result was a net profit of 172 million francs of which 121 million were distributed.

However, the value of the direct investments abroad does not lie exclusively in the distributed profits of the subsidiary companies. It also lies, among other things, in the fact that research, which today is of such enormous importance, can be placed on a broader basis. For 1968, Ciba reported 233 million francs for research expenditures; those reported by Sandoz amounted to 176 million. In the case of Hoffmann-La Roche it has been surmised that these expenditures were at the level of 300 million francs. Research expenditures of the seven big concerns are probably in the order of magnitude of 900 million francs. Research is being conducted in the affiliated companies of the concerns as well as in the parent firms. On the distribution of the research expenditures only Ciba furnishes information in some detail. In 1968, 127 million francs were spent by the parent company and 106 million by the subsidiaries. Ciba does research not only in its important affiliates in England and in the United States, but in Italy as well. As it proved difficult to transfer the profits of the subsidiary companies in India, Ciba decided to set up a laboratory and Indian chemists are now doing research with remarkable success. Results of research are being transferred in lieu of cash. In the case of Hoffmann-La Roche, affiliated firms in England and in the United States are active in research; in fact, most of the research conducted in the concern is probably being done abroad at this time. The concern is about to create two institutes for basic research in the United States. The Sandoz concern does research in Basel and in Hanover, U.S.A. Not long ago, the Sandoz Research Institute Ltd. was founded in Vienna; in the future, part of the Sandoz research is to be conducted there. Alusuisse has a 45% financial interest in the Istituto Sperimentale dei Metalli Leggeri in Milan, which devotes itself entirely to research. The Brown, Boveri Corporation in Mannheim has recently started cooperating with Krupp in the field of reactor research, and Nestlé in cooperation with Standard Oil, is engaged in basic research with the objective of securing food supply in the long run. Thanks to the direct investments abroad it is possible to utilize the experience of foreign countries and substantially to increase the research potential.

Moreover, by taking care of licenses and overhead costs of parent firms, the affiliated companies help to finance the research in which the parent companies are engaged. In some cases it seems that all research of the parent company is being financed that way; in other instances, the subsidiary companies make a major contribution. Licenses are being granted to outsider firms, too. This is so in the case of Geigy. Hoffmann-La Roche farms out production in Japan on a license basis. These are only a few examples. The story of the cooperation between parent company and affiliated firm goes even further, as frequently there is a meaningful division of labor between parent company and subsidiary. For example, the parent company or some other center of production may turn out the semifinished products, and the affiliated companies then process them into finished articles. This seems to be particularly true in the case of Hoffmann-La Roche. As we have seen, this concern, besides its numerous chemical plants, maintains 35 establishments producing finished articles. So we may well say that without the direct investments abroad the high costs of research that are necessary nowadays could hardly be borne. And the research of today means survival in the future.

From the viewpoint of the economy as a whole, the revenues of the affiliated companies represent invisibles that are of great importance for Switzerland as items offsetting the deficit in the balance of trade. It is not quite easy to trace this source of income as most of the firms do not publish any reports on it. From the annual reports of Nestlé we can gather that in 1967 the invisibles amounted to 288 million francs. In 1968 they had risen to 303 million. In the case of the other companies we know the earnings of the concerns to the extent that they are being published in the income statements. In 1967 they reached the level of 168 million francs, of which some 140 million may have originated abroad. The sum of all invisibles—licenses, contributions to cover overhead expenses, dividends, interest on short-term investments—may be estimated at some 570 million francs for the six concerns (Nestlé excluded), so that the invisible earnings of all seven concerns would amount to roughly 870 million francs. This is a substantial contribution to Switzerland's balance of payments on current account.

7. The General Economic Significance of Switzerland as a Financial Center and the International Interlocking of Capitals

Switzerland, which has no raw material deposits and whose agricultural production can supply only about two thirds of what is required to feed her population must rely on the import of raw materials and foodstuffs. As a result the balance of trade normally closes with a deficit. Ever since 1961 the annual deficits have exceeded 2 billion francs; from 1962 to 1965 they even exceeded the 3 billion mark. The quinquennium 1961-1965 produced a total deficit of 17 billion francs. The year 1969 closed with a deficit of 2.7 billion. In the postwar period the labor force of Switzerland was no longer sufficient to handle the required volume of production. So foreign workers had to be brought into the country. These workers transfer part of their savings to their homelands. Even those who just commute across a frontier to work on Swiss territory consume most of their wages abroad. All this means a drain of about 1.6 billion annually on the balance of payments on current account. To offset the deficit in the balance of trade as well as the transfers effected by the foreign workers, the Swiss economy needs invisible incomes. So far the biggest of these invisibles was tourist traffic which since 1964 yielded an annual surplus of more than 1.5 billion francs.

In the postwar era the role Switzerland has been playing as a financial center of the kind we have described in the preceding chapter has become the most important source of invisible income in the Swiss balance of payments on current account. The overall picture is presented in the following paragraphs:

(a) The earnings on *Swiss capital invested in foreign assets* may be estimated as follows:

The portfolio investments by private individuals and groups, including investment trusts, financial companies, banks, and holding companies, has been estimated by us at 1440 million francs. The estimate is largely based on an agreement about double taxation and on other indicators.

The amount of Swiss loans to foreigners in the form of bonds issued on the Swiss capital market (including indirect capital export via financial companies such as Eurofima, Pirelli S.A., and others) can be computed fairly accurately. At the end of 1968 the amount of these loans still outstanding was 7640 million francs. The loans to foreign financial companies having headquarters in Switzerland amounted to 942 million francs. The total thus adds up to 8582 million francs. On the basis of an average rate of interest of 4.88% we arrive at earnings of 419 million francs. Assuming that 40% of the loans to foreigners abroad were in foreign hands, whereas the loans to foreign financial companies with headquarters in Switzerland were subscribed almost exclusively by Swiss nationals, then a net income of approximately 270 million francs results. The earnings from the foreign portfolios of the investment trusts can be calculated more directly. At the end of 1968 these portfolios amounted to 2.56 billion. The average yield was 2.5%, which gives earnings of about 64 million francs.

The Federal Government has short-term investments abroad in the amount of 860 million francs, and long-term ones amounting to 940 million. These investments yield earnings of 76 million.

The banks have investments with the BIS, as well as single bills of exchange of this institute. These items added up to 1990 million at the end of 1968. This corresponds to earnings of 85 million francs.

Attempts to estimate earnings from direct investments abroad encounter some difficulties. In 1968 these investments probably amounted to 26 billion francs. Of these, some 2 billion are short term. Numerous investments abroad

145

Table 38.

Source of earnings	Millions of francs
Portfolio investments by private individuals, investment trusts, etc.	1,440
Direct and indirect Swiss loans to foreigners	419
Investments abroad by Federal Government	76
Investments by the banks with BIS	85
Direct investments of industry	540
Liquid funds invested on foreign Money markets	80
Total	2,640

probably do not yield any income at all, either for reasons of business policy or because of transfer difficulties. Assuming that direct investments amounting to 18 billion francs yielded 3%, the result is an income of 540 million francs. Looking at the income statements of the seven big concerns with which we have dealt in Chapter 6, we find that the earnings of the concerns are in the order of magnitude of 530 million francs. It may be that these figures include licenses; on the other hand it is certain that by no means all earnings show in the income statements. So we may well regard the estimates just set forth as cautious.

Finally, there is interest income on liquid funds invested on foreign money markets. We have estimated these investments at 2 billion francs. They have probably yielded at least 80 million francs. In view of the interest rates that prevailed in 1968, this estimate may well be accepted as conservative.

All in all, then, the earnings on capital invested abroad or in foreign assets may be estimated as shown in Table 38.

(b) The *contributions of the banking system* to the balance of payments on current account has up to now been, in most cases, underestimated. It originates in interest margins earned in transactions with foreign countries; this business is voluminous—understandably so, given the existing close ties between the Swiss banks and foreign markets. The contribution originates, furthermore, in the commissions earned in the administration of foreign property, in the gold and foreign exchange business, in transactions involving the discounting of bills of exchange and in other operations. For the years 1967 and 1968 the contribution of the banks, including the National Bank, can safely be estimated to have been something between 1.2 and 1.5 billion francs. Here the high interest rates that could be obtained on the foreign money markets may well have been a decisive factor.

(c) The amount earned in the foreign business of the *private insurance companies* has been estimated by the competent commission at 248 million francs for 1967 and at 280 million for 1968.

(d) As we have seen, the *foreign holding companies* operating in Switzerland seem to have contributed, in the form of taxes and expenses, something between 180 and 200 million francs.

(e) With respect to the *big industrial concerns* we stated that there were invisibles amounting to some 870 million francs, but this sum includes 620 million which we had already accounted for under the item "Earnings on Capital Investments." Thus an amount of 250 million francs remains, representing payments for licenses and administration expenses of the big concerns. Swiss industry as a whole has much larger incomes from licenses. But our purpose here is not to build up a national income statement but merely to estimate the contribution of the role played by Switzerland as a financial center (including the role played by the seven big industrial concerns).

Summing up, the contribution of the various financial sources to Switzerland's balance of payments on current account in 1968 was as follows:

	Millions of francs
Earnings on capital investments	2,640
Banking system	1,350
Foreign holding companies	180
Insurance companies	280
Licenses and payments for overhead expenditures of the big concerns	250
Total	4,700

But the balance of payments on current account has negative items, too. Those partly offsetting the earnings on capital investments have been entered in the official estimates with 285 million francs for 1967. In deriving this figure, the incomes from interest on loans in Swiss francs were entered "net." In our computation we must therefore set an additional sum of 150 million on the negative side. In order to allow for possible sources of error, it is probably necessary to enter outflowing interest and dividend payments with 450 to 500 million francs.

Since commodity trade and the remittances of the foreign workers have "burdened" the balance of payments in 1967 to the tune of 4.2 billion francs, we may say that the activities of Switzerland as a financial center, in the order of

Table 39. Earnings from Capital Investments by Regions (Millions of Francs)

Region	(1) Foreign securities (excluding those of column (3)) Total (largely estimated)	(2) Held by investment funds	(3) Foreign bonds issued on Swiss capital market	(4) Investments of Federal Government	(5) Direct investments by industry	(6) Total
			Type of capital investment			
EEC	770	(13)	124	28	166	1,088
EFTAᵃ	190	(12)	120	2	92	404
Rest of Europe	16	(1)	2	—	2	20
North America	381	(37)	79	22	180	662
Central and South America	60	—	7	—	60	127
Australia	6	—	14	—	10	30
Rest of world	17	—	6	—	30	53
	1,440	(63)	352	52	540	2,384

ᵃIncluding sterling area and South Africa.

148

magnitude we have estimated, are able approximately to offset these deficit items. This would mean that tourist traffic, transportation of goods, and other services have produced a surplus in the balance of payments on current account.

Our figures have not been compiled and arranged in the same way as that of the official balance of payment estimates and so they are not strictly comparable with the latter. Thus the official balance of payments statistics includes interest margins earned by the banks (about 1.9 billion in 1968) in the category "Earnings on Capital Investments," whereas the incomes of the banks from commissions are accounted for under "Other Services." Besides these differences in presentation, the total earnings we derived are somewhat higher than those in the official estimates. This is because we believe that the contribution of the banking system, the earnings from private capital investments, and the earnings from direct investments abroad have hitherto been underestimated.

The regional distribution of capital earnings can only be approximated. We obtain something like the picture shown in Table 39.

It may be of interest to compare the earnings of the Swiss financial center with those of the largest European financial center, known as the "City of London." In its Quarterly Report for December, 1968, the Bank of England essayed estimates for Britain. The Bank has grouped the earnings in a way somewhat different from the way we have grouped them on the preceding pages. In particular, transit trade and the earnings of ship brokers have been included. Confronting the English figures with comparable Swiss data, the picture of Table 40 emerges.

Table 40.

England	1967 Million pound sterling	1967 Million francs	Switzerland	1968 Million francs
Banking	22	230	Banks	1,350
Insurance	135	1,390	Insurance	280
Merchanting (1965 to 1967)	35	360	Transit trade	210
Brokerage	33	340		
Investment trusts, funds	37	380	Investment trusts, financial companies holding companies	304
Total	262	2,700		2,144

The English merchanting, which in the average of the years 1965-1967 yielded 35 million pound sterling, has its counterpart in the earnings of our transit trade firms. These were entered with 210 million in the balance of payments for 1968. The figures, to be sure, are not strictly comparable; in England as well as in Switzerland they were difficult to ascertain. There is no Swiss counterpart to the English item "Brokerage."

In England, banks and insurance companies are contributing 1620 million francs to the balance of payments; Swiss earnings by these two groups are about as high (1630 million francs), but with the difference that in England the insurance companies, and in Switzerland the banks, contributed most of the total. It is not surprising that the contribution of the insurance companies has much more weight in England than in Switzerland. After all, England is still considered the most efficient insurance center, especially in hull insurance.

More surprising is the observation that the Swiss banks earn more income from abroad than the English banks. The explanation lies in the fact that transactions aiming at profits from interest margins closed with a deficit in the case of the English banks (revenues of 96 million pound sterling and expenditures of 97 million), whereas in Switzerland this line of business yields a sizable surplus. Here we must remember that England has a large domestic money market on which funds originating elsewhere can be invested, whereas the Swiss banks must invest a large portion of their liquid funds on foreign money markets. Moreover, in Switzerland differences in rates of interest as between the homeland and the rest of the world operate to the advantage of the banks; in England they work to their disadvantage. Hence in England the income the banks are deriving from abroad is confined to what is called "Services" (23 million pound sterling), which category is roughly comparable with Swiss "Commissions." But even here the earnings of the Swiss banks are higher than those of the London City, because the Swiss banks are being entrusted with the administration of huge foreign fortunes and also because the gold and foreign exchange business is not hampered by any regulations. Nevertheless we surmise, as does the Bank of England, that the estimate for Great Britain falls short of the actual level.

The English investment trusts, unit trusts, and pension funds receive 37 million pound sterling annually from abroad, whereas the revenue received from abroad by the Swiss investment funds and financial companies is only about 124 million francs. On the other hand there is no English counterpart item to the 180 million francs that the Swiss receive from foreign holding companies.

If we take into account only the earnings of the financial and insurance institutes, leaving aside transit trade and broker transactions, we find that there is little difference between what the two financial centers are earning from abroad.

Income from capital invested abroad—we have estimated this income at 2140 million francs net for Switzerland—is not, in England, counted as income of the City. Despite the huge indebtedness which England had to incur in the last few years as a result of the deficits in her balances of payments on current account, this income was still 410 million pound sterling in 1967, the private sector contributing 583 million and the public sector closing with a deficit of 173 million. Most of this income originates in direct investments. England's net earnings from capital invested abroad are thus roughly double those of Switzerland, and so London may still be regarded as the most important center of Europe. The amazing thing is the fact that little Switzerland has come as close to the English figures as she actually did.

The degree to which capital investments are connecting the Swiss economy with other countries is reflected in the international investment position of Switzerland as shown, with the author's earlier estimates for 1960 and 1965, in Table 41.

For 1968 the assets have been entered 52 billion higher and the liabilities 22 billion higher than the corresponding figures for 1965. These increases are not only due to the intervening growth, but also to new estimates. The position of the banks shows the biggest change, with an increase of 16 billion francs on the assets side and one of about 12 billion on the liabilities side. This reflects the steadily increasing intensity of the connection of the Swiss banking system with foreign economies. We have already described this phenomenon.

The *currency reserves* were reported to have been at the level of 16,950 million francs at the end of 1968. This includes 3 billion that were taken in by the banks over the year end on a swap basis. This amount may be deducted from the currency reserves, but in that case it should be added to the assets of the banks. As these amounts are only temporarily deposited with the central bank, it is justifiable to account for them in the balance sheets of the banks. Besides the currency reserves, the Bank of Issue maintains some other foreign assets, namely, United States Treasury bonds in Swiss francs, known as Roosa bonds, amounting to 1442 million francs and an amount due by the Bank of England, which originated in actions taken to support the pound but had shrunk to 108 million francs by the end of 1968. The two items thus add up to 1550 million francs.

As far as the *banks* are concerned, we have assets of 34.4 billion francs (if the amounts originating in swaps are included) and liabilities of 28.8 billion, leaving a surplus of 5.6 billion francs. However, the investments with the Bank for International Settlements and the single bills of exchange of this institute should be added to the foreign investments of the banks, since the counterpart assets are situated abroad. At the end of 1968 the deposits with BIS amounted to 470 million, and the single bills of exchange, to 1520 million, adding up to 1990 million francs.

Table 41. The International Investment Position of Switzerland (In Millions of Francs)

	1968	1965	1960
Assets:			
Currency reserves			
Gold and foreign exchange[a]	13,950	12,350	9,850
Short-term claims			
Private:			
Due to banks	34,400	18,300	7,800
Banks' deposits with BIS	470	650	–
BIS single bills of exchange	1,520	400	–
Public:			
Short-term investments of Federal Government, incl: Roosa bonds and investments with BIS and World Bank	860	1,080	1,200
Foreign treasury notes and deposits protected from exchange rate fluctuations with foreign central banks	1,550	860	–
Long-term claims			
Foreign bonds issued on Swiss capital market incl. indirect capital exports via Eurofima, Pirelli, etc.)	8,600	6,200	3,850
Credits granted by Federal Government	940	1,000	1,150
Swiss portfolios of foreign securities:			
Investment trusts 2,600			
Private 32,400	35,000	15,700	13,000
Direct investments (excluding insurances)	26,000	17,500	10,000
Insurances (Assets)	7,200	6,000[b]	4,500[b]
Real estate and other assets	1,200	p.m.	p.m.
	131,690	80,040	51,350

[a]Excluding swap operations; [b] p.m. = pro memoria.

	1968	1965	1960
Liabilities			
Short-term indebtedness of banks	28,800	16,900	7,000
Foreign holdings of foreign bonds issued on			
Swiss capital market	3,000	2,000	1,000
Foreign portfolios of Swiss securities	9,500	5,000	5,000
Foreign direct investments in Switzerland	4,000	2,000	1,500
Insurances (liabilities)	5,700	4,500	3,500
Foreign-owned real estate and mortgage claims			
in Switzerland	7,000	6,000	3,000
	58,000	36,400	21,000

Other short-term investments are Roosa bonds owned by the Federal Government (480 million francs) and investments of the Federal Government with BIS and the World Bank (383 million), together roughly 860 million francs.

As for long-term investments, we find foreign bonds issued on the Swiss capital market (bonded Swiss loans to foreigners in Swiss francs), including indirect investments of this kind via international finance corporations with headquarters in Switzerland. These amount to 8.6 billion francs.

Into the category of long-term credits granted by the Federal Government fall four electrification loans amounting to about 600 million francs, investments in the German steel industry, and a remnant of the "clearing billion," all in all 940 million francs.

The Swiss *portfolio investments* we had estimated, conservatively, at 15.7 billion francs for 1965. For 1968 we have assumed 35 billion francs on the basis of recent investigations (cf. above, p. 116). In this total, investment trusts account for 2600 million, and private investors, including banks, financial companies, and holding companies, account for the rest. Based as it is on new calculations, this estimate is not comparable with those of 1960 and 1965.

The direct investments of industry, which we set at 17.5 billion for 1965, should be raised for the seven big concerns from 12 to 19 billion francs. The other investments abroad, which we estimated at 5.5 billion for 1965, have probably not risen in the same proportion. Even so, it is quite possible that there was an increase of about 30%, from 5.5 to 7 billion. We may therefore estimate that at the end of 1968 the direct investments amounted to 26 billion francs.

We have set the foreign assets of the insurance companies at 7.2 billion francs. Real estate, which in the preceding discussions we have mentioned only *pro memoria*, can be entered, on the basis of estimates made in banking quarters, with 1.2 billion francs. The investment in real estate abroad is partly agriculture. Thus quite a number of vineyards in the Veltlin Valley is in Swiss ownership. In this group we must include lots owned by the Federal Government for the accommodation of diplomatic representations, as well as real estate that had been part of an inheritance or had become the property of mortgage creditors, and, finally, many vacation homes outside the frontiers.

On the *liabilities* side we find debts owed by the banks amounting to 28.8 billion francs. We find foreign holdings of those foreign bonds issued on the Swiss capital market in Swiss francs; these we have estimated to be 3.0 billion francs. Foreign portfolios of Swiss securities, estimated to have been 5 billion in 1960 and 1965, may well have risen in the meantime to 9.5 billion francs as a result of the raise in the values of recently acquired securities as quoted on the stock exchange. Account must be taken of the fact that foreigners hold mostly stock of banks and big concerns, the quotations of which have risen by 60% between 1965 and 1968. For foreign direct investments we enter 4 billion francs in order to allow for some recent acquisitions and some appreciation.[17] The actuarial liabilities we have set at 5.7 billion. Real estate owned by foreigners has probably increased by 1 billion francs from 1965 to 1968. Indications suggesting this estimate are furnished by the permit procedure, prescribed since 1964, for the acquisition of real estate by foreigners.

So we find that the country's international investment position closes with total assets of 131.7 billion francs and total liabilities of 58 billion francs, leaving a surplus of 73.7 billion francs.

The United States, which have the largest volume of foreign assets, reports total assets of 147 billion dollars and total liabilities of 81 billion dollars for the end of 1968. Assets thus exceeded liabilities by 66 billion dollars. Per head of the population, the surplus is 325 dollars in the United States and 2850 dollars in Switzerland.

Although these figures purport to measure assets and liabilities in Switzerland's international investment position, they do not measure the full extent to which Switzerland as a financial center is linked to the rest of the world. Thus foreign holding companies have been excluded from these figures, for the amounts involved here—well over 10 billion francs—are merely transitory items. Nor does the balance sheet include the foreign property administered by the Swiss banks for their foreign customers. Here the Swiss banks act merely as trustees, and the amounts involved are therefore outside the investment position of the country.

In this way Switzerland, with her financial subcenters Zurich, Basel, and Geneva, has in the postwar period grown into a financial center that today ranks third after New York and London. She owes this development, and her ability to maintain the attained position, primarily to the neutrality of the country in the two great world wars, to the stability of the Swiss franc, to the central location of the country, to the multilinguality of the population, to the confidence of the surrounding world in the Swiss banks and insurance companies, to the stable political conditions in the country, and to the healthy state of her public finances which makes it feasible to keep taxes within tolerable limits. However, Switzerland would not have attained her present position as a financial center without the initiative and the enterprising spirit of the big industrial firms, the insurance companies, and the banks.

[17]On the basis of a private inquiry, Kurt Peyer estimates that the foreign direct investments in Switzerland amounted to 3.8 billion francs at the end of 1968, the most important components being investments in distributing establishments of the oil concerns (1.5 billion), and in the textile industry (700 million). The statistics of the United States list American direct investments in Switzerland in the amount of 1436 million dollars, but this includes 624 million investments in holding companies and 470 million investments in trade firms (*Survey of Current Business,* U.S. Department of Commerce, No. 10, October, 1969).

We have seen, furthermore, that Switzerland as a financial center is not an accidental product of the postwar era, but is rooted in a tradition that can be traced back to the beginnings of banking. And we have seen that the buildup of the center was repeatedly interrupted by serious setbacks.

There are probably few countries that are connected with the surrounding world as closely and in as many ways as is Switzerland. She is therefore greatly interested in stable political and monetary conditions. So her general policy is oriented toward peace and understanding between nations, and her monetary policy is oriented toward cooperation with other countries. Just as a business firm can only maintain itself if it renders useful services, so Switzerland will be able to maintain her position as a financial center only if she renders services to the surrounding world in some capacity or other—as an intermediary in capital transactions, as a provider of insurance, as an administrator of property, as a financial trustee, as a supplier of capital in the form of direct investments. Most important of all, the country will again and again have to prove its willingness to help in currency crises and to give a helping hand to less developed countries. Switzerland will have to prove this willingness because her own well-being depends in large measure on the well-being of the surrounding world.